D1272073

THE MYSTERY OF GOD'S LOVE

'In this is charity; not as though we had loved God, but because he hath first loved us, and sent his Son to be propitiation for our sins.'

(1 John 4, x.)

THE MYSTERY OF GOD'S LOVE

by

DOM GEORGES LEFEBVRE, O.S.B.

SHEED & WARD—NEW YORK

Nihil obstat Joannes M. T. Barton, S.T.D., L.S.S.
Imprimatur Georgius L. Craven, *Vic. Gen,*
Westmonasterii, die 6a. March, 1961

The Nihil obstat and imprimatur are a declaration that a book or pamphlet is considered to be free from doctrinal or moral error. It is not implied that those who have granted the Nihil obstat and Imprimatur agree with the contents, opinions or statements expressed.

This book was first published in France, under the title *Le Mystère de la Divine Charité,* by Les Editions du Cerf in 1957.

Library of Congress Catalog Card Number: 61-10173

Manufactured in the United States of America

Acknowledgements

The extracts from St John of the Cross are quoted by kind permission of Messrs Burns Oates & Washbourne, and are taken from his *Complete Works*, published by them in 1947, and translated by E. Allison Peers.

The extracts from St Teresa of Avila are from the *Complete Works*, (Sheed & Ward, 1946) translated by E. Allison Peers.

Contents

Preface

God is love, and he invites us to enter into the mystery of his love—this is the central truth of Christian Revelation and its entire sum. In the light of this truth we are able to grasp what our attitude to God should be and learn how to prepare ourselves for the work of his grace in our soul.

For this is the work of an infinitely merciful love that in our weakness shows its power, adapting itself to this weakness and bending down to tread with us our lowly ways. It is a work of love, which makes known the essential things it requires of us; and these find their key expression in Christ's commandment "Love one another" and in the example of his death on the Cross, where he demonstrated that suffering reveals its deepest meaning only in the light of divine love.

The Gift of Love

CHAPTER I

The Father loves you

In that day, you shall ask in my name; and I say not to you that I will ask the Father for you. For the Father himself loveth you, because you have loved me and have believed that I came out from God.
(John 16, 26-27)

THE revelation that Christ brings is of God's love for us, yet the words he uses to deliver this message seem charged with mystery: 'the Father himself is your friend, since you have become my friends, and have learnt to believe me'. God's love is a response to our love for Christ and to our faith in him. There are many other passages where the Gospels intimate how closely linked are the love with which the Father loves us and Christ's love for his disciples—linked so closely that they seem to be one. In Christ, it is the Father himself who loves us. This is not any sort of union, not like the mere union of two hearts joined in the same feeling. It is a mystery far more profound, which we glimpse in words such as these:

All that the Father giveth to me shall come to me; and him that cometh to me, I will not cast out. Because I came down from heaven, not to do my own will but the will of him that sent me. Now this is the will of the Father who sent me that of all that he hath given me I should lose nothing; but should raise it up again in the last day.

(John 6, 37-39)

There is no doubt that the initiative comes from the Father. He calls us to enter into the mystery of his love. But by calling us he gives us to Christ, to whom he has entrusted the fulfilment of his plans for us. And Christ shows us that the work entrusted to him comes beyond doubt, in the first place, from the Father who sent him, whose will he does—and yet, no less truly, it is his own work also. It is Christ who saves, Christ who gives life; Christ watches, that none whom the Father has given into his care should be lost; and it is he who will crown the entire work in the glory of the resurrection.

And this is the will of my Father that sent me: that every one who seeth the Son and believeth in him may have life everlasting.

(John 6, 50.)

'The Father and I are one.' This solemn affirmation—so clear that the Jews accused him of blasphemy, 'thou who art a man, dost pretend to be God', and tried to stone him—this solemn affirmation of his unity with the Father is made at the end of a discourse in which the Saviour draws a parallel between his love for his sheep and the love of the Father who gave them into his care:

My sheep hear my voice; and I know them; and they follow me. And I give them life everlasting; and they shall not perish for ever. And no man shall pluck them out of my hand. That which my Father hath given me is greater than all; and no one can snatch *them* out of the hand of my Father. I and the Father are one.

(John 10, 27-30.)

Christ's love for his sheep is seen as something absolute, something intrinsically precious, having in itself a capacity to save: 'I give them everlasting life. They can never be lost.' For the love of the Father and the love of the Son an identical phrase is used: 'No man shall pluck them out of my hand . . . no one can snatch them out of the hand of my Father.' Christ's love is not distinct from the Father's; it is not simply a reflection of, or a radiance from, the Father's; it contains the Father's love entirely. It bears all the might of his love, against which nothing can prevail.

And so the oneness of Christ and his Father is revealed to us in this manifestation of their love for us. We see that, in loving us, their will is one; yet this unity of will leaves room for that mutual understanding and sympathy which is their love for each other; an understanding the more profound, a love the more intimate, because they spring from that radical identity of being whose mystery is beyond our comprehension.

Christ revealed a further aspect of this mystery in his last discourse with his disciples. The time had come for him to leave them, yet his work was still unfinished: 'I have yet many things to say to you, but you cannot bear them now.' 'The Spirit of truth' who was to come would teach the Apostles 'all truth' (John 16, 13). 'He will teach you all things and bring all things to your mind whatsoever I shall have said to you' (14, 26). But 'he shall not speak of himself; for what things soever he shall hear, he shall speak (16, 15). But still it is from Christ that the disciples will receive what the Spirit brings them: 'he shall glorify me; because he shall receive of mine and show it to you' (16, 14). They will receive it from Christ, not because it belongs to him, but because it belongs to the Father: 'All things whatsoever the Father hath are mine. Therefore I said that he shall receive of mine and show it to you' (16, 15).

This passage, which reveals in terms laden with mystery the intimate unity of the three divine Persons, is concerned also with our salvation; it is in the fulfilment of this common task of salvation that their unity makes itself known.

Moreover, the sole aim of their common task is that we may share in this unity; and so we see clearly that this divine mystery, of which we are allowed a glimpse, is not something strange and wondrous, not simply something to dazzle the mind. It is a mystery of life, a mystery of love, of that love which is in God, which unites God to God in the impenetrable mystery of the Trinity, which is revealed to us in the common plan of the three Persons to let us share with them, and to admit us into their intimacy.

> ... that they may be one, as we also are ... as thou, Father, in me, and I in thee; that they also may be one in us; that the world may believe that thou hast sent me. And the glory which thou hast given me, I have given to them; that they may be one, as we also are one, I in them and thou in me; that they may be perfect in one; and the world may know that thou hast sent me and hast loved them, as thou hast also loved me.
>
> (John 17, 11 and 21-23.)

This revelation, made to us in Christ, that God is love and that he wants to bring us into the mystery of his love, stands at the centre of all Christian life.

Christ brought us the reality of this love which is in him and which is the love of the Father bending down towards us.

The mystery of love

No words can better express what the mystery of the Holy Trinity tells us of the inmost nature of God than those of St John the Apostle: 'God is Love.'

Consequently, our whole knowledge of God, the notion we have of his transcendence and of the relationship that we are able to have with him, take on new meaning.

To the philosopher, the ultimate reason for God's transcendence is the total independence of his being: his is a necessary being, which exists because of the demands of his own nature; he is the absolute, first being.

In the eyes of faith, the transcendence of God makes sense because God is love, his whole perfection is love. God's perfection thereby surpasses and overshadows every other greatness; not only does it surpass human grandeur, but it is something quite different; hence it can be at one and the same time at the farthest remove from us, in its splendour, and yet very close to us, in the loving intimacy into which it leads us.

God is infinitely removed from our wretchedness because he is infinitely perfect, yet infinitely close to it, for his perfection is a perfection of love, of love so powerful that our littleness cannot obstruct it.

Infinitely distant, yet infinitely close—perhaps it is in

the contrast of these two extremes that we may best see what it is that constitutes the transcendence, the distinctly divine nature, of his greatness.

This is where the mystery of the Trinity shows, in a new and more revealing aspect, the inexhaustible fullness which is in God; it reveals that his life is the life of love, the only one in which the most essential yearnings of love can be realized to the full.

For love tends towards perfect unity, towards identification with the beloved, yet in such a way that the beloved must remain a separate entity in order to remain the object of love: in the strict sense of the words, it is not possible to love oneself. Love is a giving. With its whole being it turns towards the other, it forces us out of ourselves.

So, in the very idea of love there is a sort of internal contradiction which possibly gives us an inkling that we are dealing here with too exalted a reality for the world in which we live, a sublime reality, completely divine, which can really only exist in God; in him these opposites are reconciled in a mystery of which we are allowed a glimpse.

The intimate life of the Trinity shows us that in God this yearning of love is entirely satisfied: the three divine Persons are one in the unity of the one nature, which is possessed by each in so far as each communicates it to the others, in so far as each gives it and receives it in an exchange of love. And nothing distinguishes them one from another but those very relationships which bind them to each other in this exchange which is all love.

This is the union in which grace gives us a share. Grace and grace alone can bring us to this mystery of love; it is to be found only in God; and we cannot look for it outside God without stumbling against the impossibility of really opening ourselves to the beloved and knowing his inmost thoughts, without ending with that feeling of isolation in which every effort to find real communion away from him, who alone is the centre of unity, comes to grief.

Grace is God's gift of himself to us. Of course everything is a gift from God, but of all these gifts there is only one in which God truly gives himself, and that we call grace. God is present wherever the fruits of his generosity are to be found; but himself he gives only to the sanctified soul; in that soul he lives, making it radiant with the life that is in him, that life which will be revealed in its full glory in heaven, but which already gives life to the soul: it already possesses the inner principle, God is present before it, as though giving himself so that the soul may know and love him, as though giving it the ability to enjoy him as its only good.

This new life is a life received: the soul owes its existence in grace to the absolute gift of God, the gift of love, in which the gift is God himself.

It is an absolute gift; the soul possesses it only in so far as it has received it, it lives in the knowledge of its complete gratuitousness, in the knowledge of being all that it is by virtue of a completely gratuitous favour, which makes it so entirely dependent upon him whom it loves.

A lover wants nothing in him to exist independently of his love; he wants to live only for the beloved, and only as long as his life depends on the beloved. God's gift of grace is an answer to this longing, it refashions the soul, from it the soul takes a new being. The soul loves its God, but this is not only a free choice of its own will. Its choice is simply the expression of a much deeper truth, proceeding from its inmost depth, from the life within it which has made it a new creature, and which is a gift of love.

And, if men can achieve genuine union with each other, if it is given them to break down that isolating wall that shuts each off from the other, then this will be through their common participation in that pure, real love. To love each other means to love God together, to share in that oneness which, without God, we cannot possess. For God alone can enter so intimately into our inmost heart, knowing us more truly than we know ourselves. There can be no union that is not in harmony with the unique centre of unity. There can be no love except in him, for he is love.

To love God is to receive the gift of his love. Human love can only be an echo, awakened in our hearts because God has spoken first. It is precisely because it is an echo that our love can be so profound, reverberating with all the wealth of that divine word of which it is simply a reproduction; blossoming into an act of complete faith that expresses our feeling of completely belonging to him who, in giving us his love, has taken possession of our very being.

The beatific vision in which we shall know perfect union with God and full participation in his life will be not simply looking at him, not simply contemplation, but a surge of the whole soul, complete belonging, love; and that is what is already happening when we make an act of faith with our whole soul, when we give ourselves and know ourselves to be utterly possessed by him towards whom our whole being aspires, him in whom we find our rest.

In the act of faith there is already something of the beatific vision.

We are emptied of everything, nothing remains but the joy of abiding in the will of God, we desire nothing but to see his will accomplished in us, everything in us is pliant to his will; it is not simply that we know he desires our good, but something much truer and more profound: his will is our only good and our only joy lies in surrendering ourselves to it entirely.

The response to love

God is love, he desires all our relations with him to be on the plane of love, of love freely given. Our proof of the absolute gratuitousness of this gift is that, to obtain it, all we have to do is to desire it: that is the only response he asks of us.

St Thomas, enquiring why it is that, the more burning their love at the hour of death, the more clearly will the elect see God in heaven, answers that as desire springs from love, so those whose love is more fervent will desire more strongly and will therefore be more abundantly rewarded.

So, we will be judged on the strength of our desire;

when we appear before him, God will greet us not as a severe master demanding a strict account, but as a Father who wants only to give, to give each of us what he asks for; and they will receive nothing to whom there is nothing that he can give, since, being without love, they desire nothing.

The only purpose of our life then, is that the desire for God should grow in our heart until it is so strong that when we appear before him we can hold it out to him, as the only thing that entitles us to the quite gratuitous gift of his love. That is why the important consideration in this life is not to find God—or to think that we have found him—but never to grow weary of seeking him. And perhaps that is the real meaning of those lives which have been an unwearying pursuit of God, of a God who seemed impossible to reach—pursuit in anxiety, in temptations to discouragement—of those souls who have never known the feeling of having found peace. And yet their lives have been filled with constant burning desire that nothing has been able to quench; and, when the time comes for them to offer it to God for his reward, then will they see how much they owe to all those difficulties that were never able to overcome their perseverance.

The first thing that is asked of us is fidelity; fidelity best shows that our desire is sincere, that it is not a mere, fleeting, emotional state but a profound intention of the will strengthened by love, proof against the weariness of difficult times, when God is hidden and the monotony of the daily round weighs heavily, proof too against all those myriad earthly joys that try to draw us to easy pleasures which mislead our thirst for happiness without being able to satisfy it; an intention that will, by its very tenacity, gradually grow stronger, struggling without cease against the obstacles that lie in longings and joys that want to take up a little of our heart, a little of that strength, every ounce of which must be put at the service of the unique love to which it has given itself.

Not of course, that we could ever dream of arriving at a state where we no longer had any preferences, any hopes or fears; we are still human, and engaged in the turbulence of human life. But may this desire for God, which is also a source of joy, since we know that we need only persevere in it to reach its goal, be so strong and so assured that, without actually excluding everything else, we will at least be able to renounce all other things if that is asked of us, without losing any of our peace or ceasing to be happy.

Desire for God is our most precious good; we must guard it jealously, keeping it free from those encroachments that could rob it of its strength. For it is, so to speak, a magnet in our soul, attracting grace. God cannot leave unanswered a desire with which he has himself inspired us. What is more, he has told us: 'So many athirst, who will not come to the water . . . come, and get food, get wine and milk free, no price to be paid' (Isaias 55, 1). It is enough to be athirst; that is all that is required. 'Those who are thirsty shall drink—it is my free gift—out of the spring whose water is life' (Apoc. 21, 6).

He had filled the hungry with good things, and sent the rich away empty-handed' (Luke I, 103). 'The rich'—they thought themselves so when they had the things of this earth, thought there was nothing left for them to desire, they were too completely satisfied with their earthly happiness to feel the need for any higher joy. God left them amidst the destitution of their plenty. But those who hunger and thirst for justice, their longing he welcomes as if it were a prayer. He is himself the inspiration of it, to the extent that he means to satisfy it. Thus it is a pledge and a promise of grace, a sign that it is part of God's plan to give us those gifts for which he makes us long.

The saints have often told us this; John of the Cross, for instance, said 'The more God wants to give us, the more demanding he makes our desires'; and it is an idea to which Thérèse of the Child Jesus was particularly attached. We come across it all the time in her writings; in the first chapter of her autobiography she says: 'There it all was, the history of my life, of my vocation; above all, of the special claims Jesus makes on my soul. He doesn't call the people who are worthy of it; no, just the people it pleases him to call.'[1]

And the mark of this call from God is that he implants in the soul a longing for his grace, with which he means to fill it to overflowing. 'Why should our Lord want us to suffer unnecessary pain? Why should he inspire me with this ambition to become a victim, if he doesn't mean to satisfy it?'[2] The thought that God wouldn't 'inspire us with ambitions that can't be realized',[3] encouraged her to aspire to holiness 'despite my littleness'. In another

[1]*Autobiography of a Saint* translated by Ronald Knox, p. 33 (Harvill, 1958).

[2]*Ibid.*, p. 221.

[3]*Ibid.*, p. 248.

place we are told that she once said: 'Would he have given me this ever increasing desire to do good on earth after my death if he did not mean to fulfil it? No, rather he would give me the inclination to rest in him.' Or again, in her act of offering 'I know, oh my God, that the more you want to give us, the more you make us long for.'

The initiative always comes from God; he loved us first; our desire can be an effective prayer because it is a response to the will to give which is in God; 'he has but one desire, which is to find souls to whom he can give' (St Teresa, *The Interior Castle,* Fourth Mansion, ch. 4).

His desire to give not only anticipates all that he could possibly desire to receive, but even exceeds it:

> it seems that there is no more to desire; but our most holy King has much more to give: He would rejoice to do nothing but give, could he find souls capable of receiving. And, as I have often said, daughters, you must never forget that the Lord is not content with giving us according to the small measure of our desires: I have noticed that myself.
>
> (St Teresa, *Conceptions of the Love of God,* vol. 11, ch. 6, p. 390.)

That is why we should never think of moderating our ambitions:

> We must have great confidence, for it is most important that we should not cramp our good desires, but should believe that, with God's help, if we make continual efforts to do so, we shall attain, though perhaps not at once, to that which many saints have reached through His favour.... His Majesty desires

> and loves courageous souls if they have no confidence in themselves but walk in humility, and I have never seen any such person hanging back on this road, nor any soul that, under the guise of humility, acted like a coward, go as far in many years as the courageous soul can in few. . . . We must always keep humility before us, so that we may realize that this strength cannot proceed from any strength of our own. But it is necessary that we should realize what kind of humility this must be, for I believe the devil does a great deal of harm to those who practise prayer by encouraging misunderstandings about humility in them so as to prevent them from making much progress.
>
> (St Teresa, *Life,* vol. 1, ch. 13, pp 74-75)

We can understand why the Church, in the prayer she asks us to say for the gift of ardent love, bids us ask for nothing but the grace of this desire, which is the pledge and the promise of all that follows from it:

> Give to our hearts an abiding love for thee; that the desires we conceive by thine inspiration may ever remain unchanged in spite of every temptation.

We do not ask God to satisfy our longings, but simply to fix them more firmly in our heart, as the sole claim we can make to the free gift of his grace.

The refusal of love

We do not stand in Gods' sight simply as servants before their master; he is love, he has willed that our dealings with him should take place on the plane of love; so if we are to understand sin, we must view it on the same plane.

Sin is not only an offence against divine justice, it is a refusal of divine love—and this makes it a far deeper mystery.

This stands out with absolute clarity in that surpassing sin, that sin which embodies the whole conception of sin, of which other sins are only a reflection—the sin of Satan.

So often it is through sheer weakness that man does not open himself to grace; but Satan shut himself off from love by an absolutely deliberate refusal sprung from his pride. He was stopped short by the first, the most essential, of love's demands: he would not enter into the mystery of charity because it is the mystery of humility. He could not bring himself to accept happiness as a gift, whereas it can never be anything else, being found only in love, love freely given, which cannot be in us without shaping us in its likeness, yet without in any way robbing us of our own nature. Receiving everything as a gift, how can we fail in the joy of pure thanksgiving to recognize that we no longer possess anything in our own right?

That is what Satan refused to accept: he wanted to owe his happiness to no one but himself, somehow to snatch his perfect nature out of the Creator's hands and possess it in complete independence, relishing it and sating himself with the cold joy of pride. He wanted to stand alone, and the only way he could do this was to enclose himself in the narrow limits of that perfection he had wanted for himself, that perfection he had thought capable of satisfying him, in which there was no room for love, but only for the aridity of self-love.

Adam's sin was the same sort of revolt—he wanted to be god-like, to choose for himself his own way of being happy, to receive his happiness from himself. This is the constantly renewed temptation of pride.

Of pride . . . or of our own weakness, which is incapable of protecting itself against easy attractions. But God, when he made man, set him in a state where he was fortified against the weakness inherent in his nature.

It is a weakness that gives us a taste for the comforts of this world; we know that they are inferior yet our senses drive us to attain them at once, to see them and touch them, while our mind struggles to raise itself to spiritual matters. We know that the things of the spirit are better and more perfect, yet only with difficulty can we gain even a vague image of them, (an image which cannot really reveal the true picture), in which they always seem far removed from us and almost entirely inaccessible.

God did not leave man to his inherent weakness; with a view to the future gift of grace, and so that everything in man's nature that grace was to animate with a new life should be amenable to its workings, he prepared the way for it with gifts of light and strength which, by strengthening reason and establishing its hold over man's sensual life, prepared both reason and feeling to respond to the movement of grace without setting any obstacle in its way.

The first man was to have handed down these privileges, that go beyond nature and yet perfect it in its own sphere, and in some way are proportionate to it, to his descendants as their claim to the right to receive that supernatural gift, in the expectation of which they were granted, that gift with which God would straightaway have endowed the soul clothed in them.

But just because this link existed between grace and these privileges, man, when by his sin he lost grace (for his revolt was an outright attack against it), was at the same moment denuded of those privileges, which existed only for grace, and had no further justification once grace was gone.

After the fall the nature that he passed on by generation was therefore stripped of any claim on grace, simply because of his wilful revolt against God, an offence against his majesty and against his love. This is how we are born in a state of revolt and under the sway of him who, having lured our first father into his disobedience, will lead us too into sins which again and again reiterate and aggravate mankind's first refusal of the love of our God.

But God, in his mercy, took pity on us and did so, moreover, to such an extent that the Church bids us reflect that, in the long run, we have gained more than we lost from the consequences of the first sin, that blessed fault which brought us such a Redeemer!

For we have been given in Christ a new right to share in the divine life, a right more precious than those of which we have been deprived. If now we are granted grace, it is not by virtue of a nature fit to receive it through the gift of integrity, but because we are one with Christ, God and man, who is our head, of whom we are members. By virtue of this stronger claim we now have on it, grace is distributed with greater abundance. On the other hand it finds us abandoned to our natural weakness; no longer is the ground prepared in advance; now it is for grace to strengthen our reason and our will, bringing them under Gods' rule, teaching them to find in that submission the power to overcome the revolts of the flesh. In this way it is possible, through the workings of grace, for order and harmony to be rebuilt in us step by step. It must gradually subdue this intractable territory into which it has come and where it meets with so many obstacles. We must prepare ourselves for the workings of grace so that, through it, everything in us will turn freely towards God, but it is grace that does the work, entering ever more deeply into our being, submitting everything to its sanctifying influence.

A more difficult task, doubtless, but also a much finer one; and since, henceforth, suffering has become love's instrument, without which it cannot achieve its work, the way lies open for God, who showers us the more abundantly with his gifts since our claim to them is so much greater, to take a far more entire possession of our soul.

To understand what divine love wants to achieve in us in this way, we cannot do better than consider the mystery of the Immaculate Conception of our Lady.

The grace given to our Lady is the saving grace merited for us by Christ on the Cross, and her claim to this gift of God's benevolence is, like ours but more eminently so, her union with Christ. This privilege, lost to man since Adam, is part of a new order; our Lady, from the first moment of her conception, received in a human nature exactly like ours the gift of grace, grace in such abundance that from that moment everything in her, being entirely subject to grace, turned in perfect harmony toward God.

What grace accomplished in Mary, in so striking a way, is just what it must gradually achieve in us, delivering us little by little from sin and the consequences of sin, until its redeeming work is complete in our soul.

Love's entreaties

God therefore condescended to stoop towards his creature; he went so far as to invite man to enter into the intimacy of God, and mankind refused this gift of love, not only by the first sin but by every sin which since then has strengthened the first and makes but one sin with it. Man has adopted an attitude, a permanent state of refusal. How was God to react to such a reception of his entirely conciliatory act of kindness? By giving us new instances of his infinite love; we had repulsed his gift, and now he pressed it upon us even more compellingly and persuasively. Sin took us away from him, so he came further in search of us. That is how man's rejection called forth God's superabundant gift.

We did not want his love; now God offered it to us in a more approachable form, brought it more within the reach of our human weakness which, intensified by sin, only really responds to material, tangible things, while we find it so difficult to bring ourselves to understand, still less to love with a love that stirs and grips the heart, this reality of the spirit. The love of God, of God supreme and transcendent . . . how can we fathom the depths of its mystery? How can we form an idea of such love, how can we realize what it may have in common with that human emotion we call by the same name? How much nearer home it becomes when we see it shining through the actions and least gestures of Christ, living in our midst a life like our own: 'through the mystery of the Word made flesh thy splendour has shone before our mind's eye with a new radiance, and through him whom we recognize as God made visible we are carried away in love of things invisible' (Preface of Our Lord's Nativity). 'We are carried away': there is a resistance in us that must be overcome; God, now, must not only invite us, he must persuade us to accept the gift of his love.

There is yet another way in which this love, through Christ, comes closer to us. Love is the very heart of the mystery of the life of God, the bond uniting the divine persons in an intimacy which, far from seeming bound to open itself for us, seems on the contrary infinitely beyond our wildest aspirations. Love is the very life of the Trinity, its own entirely personal possession; doubtless God is free to grant us a share in it, but no man on his own merits can lay any claim to it.

In Christ, God's love is already ours, made for us, asking to grow in us—not of course by virtue of its nature, but by virtue of the condition in which we see it. For love could have no other reason for assuming this condition but to give itself to us.

In other words, it was not possible for Christ to become man without *continuing* to live, in his assumed human nature, that life of love which is his in the heart of the Trinity. But neither could he assume this bond with us, make us this gift of becoming one with our human nature, unless that gift were directed towards bringing us into communion with the divine life which is in him and which he chose to live in a human nature like ours.

He willed, when he became our head, that a common bond should exist between him and us; so Christ, the Word Incarnate, God and man, has made himself our claim to receive the gift of grace which exists in him only so as to be shared with all his members.

The Incarnation was the crowning proof of divine love; was there any better way for God to show us that he does not keep his creature at a distance, any way for him to draw nearer to us, to give himself more completely, than by becoming one of us, a man among men? There seems no point to such a great offering except to bring us into the mystery of love.

But this renewed offering of love was, by itself, no longer enough; it yet remains for us to respond to it. For love is an exchange.

Of course, had God wanted our relations with him to be conducted on the plane of justice, he could have conceded that justice was by no means satisfied; and this would have prevented his mercy from forgiving the fault, without first demanding from those who were incapable of giving it, satisfaction proportionate to their offence.

But God could not allow his greatest work, the work of his love, from which spring all his other works, to be left unfinished. Yet love must have a response—it cannot exist without one—and the response must be fitting.

Man was not able to make this perfect response, capable of wiping away all trace of that first refusal, leaving no shadow on outraged love, restoring it to its first radiance. But God, in justice to himself, was obliged to stipulate that there must be no interference in the plan of his love except what was necessary to restore it to even greater heights, leaving nothing unfulfilled, but rather showing even more clearly his intention to give all that is in him to give.

That is what Christ came to do: to restore the work of divine charity not just to its former state but to an even greater perfection by offering to the Father, in the name of mankind, to which he belongs and whose head he is, a response in which nothing remains of that first refusal.

Our Lord makes good this first refusal, at the same time as he overcomes it, in his struggle to regain mankind for love which, the first time, it failed to recognize. The gift once despised is now not merely accepted; for Christ's labour to restore the reign of divine love in this world, a labour which led him to his Passion and death on the Cross,—endured so that he might overcome the power that lies in man to refuse love—was a completely satisfactory response to love; in its absolute perfection, it more than completely redeemed the offence that had been given to love.

For God's work to be really perfect, however, the whole of mankind must make this response and Christ, not content with acting for us, in our stead, must give us also the power to respond in unity with him, to make our own response through his.

Without his reparation, to which our own is joined, ours—which has some value in so far as it unites his members with him in a common offering—would be worth nothing. Our love is accepted by the Father because it is his love in which we have a part; just so our labours, our difficulties, our trials are worth something in so far as they are one with his, one with the sufferings he, our head, sharing our lot, offered for our sakes and to which, because of this common lot, we can and must join our own.

When we understand the degree to which the work of our redemption is a work of love, then the mystery of redemptive suffering will have some meaning for us. Of course it will always be a source of amazement for us that the God of all goodness could permit such misery, but if we reflect that these trials are not mere punishment, but a necessary condition of our higher vocation, then perhaps we will at least come to suspect that there does exist an answer to this dilemma.

St Paul reports this saying of our Lord: 'It is more blessed to give than to receive.' What a wealth of meaning lies in these words when they come from the mouth of God—like an avowal of love that escapes his lips, revealing the inner meaning of all our relations with him, the secret of his infinitely freely given love.

When we have tried to trace the successive stages, the repeated advances of this divine love, that has sought to discover and use every possible way of giving itself, then we should re-read those words of our Lord that St Paul has preserved from oblivion.

We learn from them to direct our longing, our prayer, our humble efforts, to this God who, going to the very extremes of love, desired to draw near and make himself approachable by becoming one of us; and this he turned into an act of mercy, a supreme effort of his infinite charity to overcome our resistance, and force us to accept the gift he holds out.

The sacrament of love

Christ is one with his members; the mystery of his life, death and resurrection will be complete only when it is fulfilled in us. Hence the mysteries of Christ are not entirely contained in the events of the few years he spent on earth as one of us. They are continued in his Church, tending in her towards their final consummation; they are present and continue their life in his mystical body and in each of its members. This is not simply an interior presence but, as with the Incarnation, it takes on an outward form, appearances under which these mysteries are offered to us in a manner adapted to the conditions of human life on earth, which is where we must live them.

We must learn first of all to recognize their presence in the most ordinary circumstances of our daily lives; that is where they take their place, in just the same sort of circumstances as Christ himself lived them. For it is not that on one side there is his own personal life, a reality entirely of God, and on another side our miserable lives clinging on to him somehow or other from the outside. In Christ, as in us, there is a purely human existence, made up of plain, ordinary things but irradiated with a divine mystery that has its being in Christ and which he allows us to live with him. If we are tempted at times to think that this is not so, and fail to understand this fundamental unity of Christ and his members, surely this is because we are too accustomed to looking at the trifling events of our daily lives from a narrow and self-centred angle, and hence they seem greatly removed from the mysteries that we contemplate in prayer, which set us on an entirely different plane? And yet it is these very mysteries that are at work in all that is most ordinary and commonplace in our lives, giving them meaning and complete reality.

So, as an aid for human weakness, Christ willed that his presence should not be entirely unseen but that we should be able to reach him by means of signs he would give us. That is what the Church is for—to be the continuation of the Incarnation of the mystery in which God offers himself to us in a way that our senses can apprehend. The Church is the sacrament of the presence of Christ, the Word Incarnate: through her priesthood and the sanctifying power that appertains to it, we know that we have grace at our disposal; the Church shows us that God's aid is always waiting for us when we need it; and so the Church enlightens for us the complete freedom of this gift of supernatural life.

Christ willed to leave us with tangible signs of his presence. His grace is offered to us through sacred actions and he himself dwells in our midst, at the centre of the sacramental order, in that one of his mysteries that contains all the others and which is our principle source of grace: the mystery of his death and resurrection.

That is the meaning of the Eucharist: Christ sacrificed for the salvation of men, returning to the Father in the glory of his resurrection, seated for ever at his side, branded with those marks that show him to be the victim of our salvation: 'the Lamb led to the slaughter' whom St John the Apostle beheld in his vision. As he is in heaven, so is he also on our altars, as victim; the appearances under which he is present among us are both the symbol and the manifestation of this state. He is really present, so that we in our turn can really offer him, just as he really offered himself for us, and can join our offering to his.

That is how, in the Eucharistic mystery, the actual sacrificial act of redemption is re-enacted and is forever present in the life of the Church, filling it with the life of divine grace that springs from it, gathering the whole Church together to offer it to its head, so that it may participate in that supreme consecration in which everything returns to the Father and is consummated in the mystery of his love.

Love's great achievement

One creature was singled out and granted the privilege of being more closely united than any other to those mysteries of Christ in which we all have a share: she lived them with him, she was a part of them, they were hers in a unique manner. We see the Blessed Virgin Mary as one with her Son, in the mind of the Father, from the very beginning of time. When, straight after the Fall, in the garden of Eden, God promised mankind a Saviour, he alluded to her whom we call the second Eve, along with the second Adam, who is Christ.

And when the time came for God's eternal plans to come to fruition, the angel bearing the message of salvation was sent to her. To her was the announcement made of the coming of the Saviour and she, in the name of all mankind, accepted the Redeemer given to us, and greeted this gift from the mercy of God with her words of consent: 'Be it done unto me.' Through her, because he is her Son, Christ is really ours, one of us, our brother, involved in the destiny of mankind whom he came to save, really and truly one with us.

Through her the Word was made flesh; and since God became man to redeem us, and because the mystery of his incarnation and the mystery of our redemption are necessarily a part of each other, the part played by Mary could not stop short with the Incarnation. Her place at the foot of the Cross was marked out. She was closely united to the drama of Calvary. She endured as her own, in her mother's heart, her Son's sufferings, those sufferings which tore us out of the grip of sin and the kingdom of Satan.

What gives her her stature in our eyes is the infinitely close union she was destined to have in the mysteries of Christ, our God and Saviour. The mother's greatness is her Son. Because she was so close to them in the mystery of his life on earth, so is she also closely concerned with the life of the Church in which his work will be fulfilled. She cannot hold herself aloof from this, because it is hers, her Son's work. She sees him in us; in each one of us, his members, she sees her own destiny being fulfilled and watches over it with a motherly eye.

That is why, at the first Pentecost, Mary was there with the apostles: she was present at the birth of the Church, just as she was to be throughout its whole life. The councils that lay down definitions of Christian faith speak of her; one of the most solemn affirmations of the divinity of Christ was the definition of the council of

Ephesus that recognized Mary's title as Mother of God.

Mary is the glory of the Church. She is one of us, a creature like us, and like us, redeemed. She has received, even more than we, God's mercy: she is all pure, immaculate, as a result of that merciful grace of salvation earned by her Son on the Cross, from which she benefited more than any other human being.

Mary is one of us and yet she is so great. So 'full of grace' that the beauty of the whole Church shines in her; the liturgy loves to take up and apply to her those scriptural images—spouse pure and without stain—in which the magnificence of the Church is proclaimed.

Mary, from all eternity a part of the Father's plan for us, chosen by him from all others to be closely linked with the work of his Son, the work of our salvation; Mary, Mother of God; redeemed like us, yet so close to Christ, so intimately concerned in his work that, in him and by him, she is such that we love to call her our hope, our life, our salvation; Mary, present in all the mysteries in which God reveals himself and gives himself to us.

To us she seems to be clothed with the radiance of the glory of God, working with him, taking part in the fulfilment of the plans of his grace and mercy. She lived the mysteries of our redemption with her Son, by her side; so deeply committed to his work was she, that she had no thought of existing for any other purpose. We might well ask ourselves what would have become of us if God had willed to give himself to us in some other way, without going so far as to become a man like us. Mary is so much a part of the economy of the Incarnation that she exists only on its account and in relation to it, and herein lies her greatness.

Yet, like us, more even than us, she is the object of divine mercy, redeemed by her Son's blood. God frees each one of us from the yoke of sin at the moment of our baptism, with a completely gratuitous generosity; greater still was the generosity by which he freed Mary from that law of sin, so that sin never left the slightest mark upon her. She, even more than we, must sing in thanksgiving the praises of the divine mercy which from age to age is shed on those who fear the Lord: *Et misericordia ejus a progenie in progenies.*

Among all the riches of divine grace it is she who gives eloquent testimony to the infinite condescension of God, who not only came down to our level in the mystery of the Incarnation but drew even closer to us, showing how greatly he wished to make himself approachable, familiar to us, by taking flesh in the womb of a virgin who, absolutely pure though she was, yet belonged to the race of sinners, who, in heaven, not only sings with the angels in praise of the grace of God but also makes one with the choir of the saints to sing for all eternity of the Lord's mercy towards mankind, redeemed with the blood of Christ.

In this woman, blessed above all women, who bore in her womb him whom we adore as our God, who loved him with a mother's love, we see how much God wanted to raise man up to himself, to draw infinitely near to his creature.

Mary, full of grace, showered with God's blessings, bears witness in our eyes to the infinite store of his goodness, shows us the intimacy to which God invites a mere creature. She is a pledge of the boundless generosity with which he bestows the gifts of his love. She calls on us to come more trustingly to him, God, who does not despise those who, in the shadow of his vastness, are but dust, whose love is mighty enough to raise us to him.

The mystery of Mary is a confirmation of the almightiness of God's love; it reveals more of the mystery of divine generosity to us; it calls us to understand more clearly what that grace which achieved such great things in her, can do in us.

The Humble Paths of Love

CHAPTER I

Renunciation and humility

God is love and, because he is love, he wants to give us a share in his life and bring us into the mystery of his love. He seeks souls that are open to grace and ready to welcome his gifts. As *The Imitation of Christ* puts it, 'the grace of the Holy Spirit seeks the humble of heart'.

'The humble of heart'—humility prepares the way for God and allows him the freedom to carry out his plan. We cannot make ourselves equal to the gift God offers us, nor worthy of it, by raising ourselves up to him. The only way to welcome it is by humbling ourselves before it, in the knowledge of our nothingness and of its absolute gratuitousness.

God himself must throw light on the holiness of the mystery he wishes to achieve in us for us to understand to what exquisite perfection our humble self-effacement must strive if we are to be responsive to grace. But we must be ready to accept his light. Every effort of renunciation we make tends in this direction; it is his light that lets us perceive just what renunciation should be, and the spirit in which we should practise it.

It is not simply that we must learn perfect self-control, which is a condition for any full development of the personality, for any fruition of man's best qualities. The pagan philosophers admired this very human ideal, but it does not go far enough for the Christian. The Christian must naturally strive to achieve self-discipline, learn to subdue his emotions, but this is for him only a means of clearing away obstacles that obstruct God's grace. Not only has grace made his efforts subserve a higher end; by giving him a new goal it has altogether changed him; now another spirit moves him, and he must ultimately achieve a much more profound transformation of himself.

We must open ourselves to divine love, which flourishes only in humility. Love is humble, since its perfection lies not in the intensity of feeling it inspires but in its purity: the purity of a soul that gives itself unsolicited, emptied, as only humility can empty it, of everything that belongs to it.

That is true of any love; how much more does it apply to the love into which God leads his creature. Christian humility should be so much more profound, since it responds to the absolute gratuitousness with which God gives us his gifts, since everything in us comes from him and belongs only to him. Not only our nature, which is his creation, belongs to him but, by an even more undeniable right, the work of his love in our soul is his. This is a divine mystery, the mystery of the freedom with which God gives, which can be realized only in purity, the sensitive purity of the absolutely humble heart.

Humility is therefore the corner stone of all Christian asceticism. Gradually it works a transformation in the heart, making it more and more responsive to the divine truth from which it must obtain its life.

God alone is able to make us see the real meaning of this virtue:

> Simplicity is strictly Christian, for the pagans, even those who have spoken highly of the other virtues, have no knowledge of it, nor of humility either; they have had good things to say about good works, liberality, prudence, constancy, but nothing at all about simplicity and humility. Our Lord himself came down from heaven to teach men about both these virtues, about both equally, since otherwise they would never have known this very necessary doctrine.
>
> St Francis de Sales,
> *Introduction to the Devout Life,* ch. 13.

Humility, said St John of the Cross, 'has the effects of love', of the presence of the Holy Spirit, of which St Paul spoke:

> Charity is patient, is kind, charity envieth not, dealeth not perversely, is not puffed up, is not ambitious, seeketh not her own, is not provoked to anger, thinketh no evil; rejoiceth not in iniquity, but rejoiceth with the truth; beareth all things, believeth all things, hopeth all things, endureth all things.
>
> (1 Cor. 13, iv-vii.)

> But the fruit of the spirit is: charity, joy, peace, patience, benignity, goodness, longanimity, mildness, faith, modesty, continency.
>
> (Gal. 5. xxii-xxiii.)

In short, love is peace; a peace made of gentleness, patience, renunciation, humility.

This purity of heart that is born of humility is reached only by a long-lasting struggle with oneself, with pride and that self-will in which pride is so firmly embedded. This struggle has nothing in common with the triumph of a soldier on the battlefield, glorying in his conquering strength. It must model itself on a different victory—the victory that Christ won on the Cross, by the acceptance of suffering and humiliation, that bore the outward mark of weakness and defeat.

By copying him, we may win this battle against self, against 'covetous nature, that prefers to receive rather than to give . . . that acts always in its own interests, for its own advantage . . . that is selfish in all its doings . . . that wants to be looked up to, and acts so as to arouse admiration and compliments'. Then will grace triumph, grace 'that is simple and humble . . . generous, and given to all men'. (*Imitation of Christ* 3, 54.)

Thus victory is achieved not so much by heroic sacrifices as by constant faithfulness to the most ordinary duties, hidden in the silence of everyday life; by the acceptance of set-backs and trials that God has sown along our way; and finally and most important, by gentleness, patience, unselfishness in our dealings with our neighbour. In that way we acquire forgetfulness of self, a condition of the love which will reveal itself to us in its most intricate subtleties. In this way the soul becomes susceptible to the most precious graces of prayer, for only in prayer, in the presence of God, can the soul realize how necessary it is to be humble before him and how sweet this humility of love is, with what peace and joy it fills the heart where it abides.

Humility leads to joy, for it sets us in the way of truth, of this one great truth, that God is love; God is charity; God gives himself freely. Everything we have comes from his infinite generosity. Nothing comes from ourselves. We can call nothing our own. Everything belongs to God and must be subject to him, left in his hands. Humility makes us live our lives by the light of this truth; through humility we take the place that belongs to us in the mystery of God's love.

To fall away from humility, from the total dependence in which it holds us, is to fall away from love, away from this mystery of God's complete generosity.

Simplicity

Perfection, being wholly inward, is a simple thing; it is not by the magnificence of the works it inspires but by the purity of intention that occasions them, that God's love is measured. And probably it is nowhere easier to achieve this purity of intention than in humble compliance with the commonplace demands of our daily round.

There we shall find the most efficacious means of working at this self-reformation. It will not be done in a day, since the obstacles that have to be overcome are not of the kind that can be removed all at once. Only a persevering attack will have an effect on them. Patience will be needed. We will be troubled at finding ourselves at the mercy of so many feelings against which it is so hard to defend ourselves, at seeing ourselves so quickly upset and downcast by such little things, such as a gesture of irritation for some petty enough cause which, nonetheless, we have not been able to overcome.

We will find very few grounds for complacency when we are brought face to face with ourselves in this way, in a struggle that makes us keenly aware of every indication of our virulent and still scarcely mortified self-love.

Of course there will not only be defeats or dubious victories in the struggle; there will be genuine triumphs too, which will afford us joy greater than any other.

Then we shall see our will set free from one of the obstacles that stood between it and God; we were restrained by the bonds that tied us to things we could not give up. Where they were concerned we were not free, we could not be deprived of them without agitation. And now, one of those chains has fallen off; we have come up against one of our customary difficulties and overcome it, almost without effort. The obstacle has yielded and there, stretching before us, we think we see the road to God. Henceforth everything seems simpler and easier.

But what made it possible for us to carry the day like this? Very often it is the unexpected outcome of a long series of defeats. No sudden act of generosity has at one blow granted us the victory. Far from it! Such a long succession of poor attempts went before it, made in the knowledge of our weakness, of our continuing inability to hold ourselves proof against feelings that are all too human, that prevent us from raising ourselves to a single, simple, spontaneous gift of self. But God was pleased with this humble evidence of good will. His grace worked in silence and today's victory, the peace that fills the heart and puts to flight the cares and anxieties of yesterday, is too clearly his work to inspire in us any feeling but humble and joyful thanksgiving.

It is even more true to say that the long process of grace is accomplished with very ordinary, very modest means; the sacrifices that occasioned it will seem little enough when we know how to guard against this temptation to self-love and self-attachment, which lends such undue importance to the slightest trial. It is important to be on our guard against this temptation, for by giving in to it we fall away from the truth and then nothing is safe for us. Then we no longer know what we should do. If we are to accept a sacrifice in the proper spirit the first thing necessary is to reduce it to its true proportions, and then simply and joyfully to make the necessary effort, an effort for which, since it is made in sincerity, the grace will be provided.

It is not so easy to do the right thing, in this way, amid the intricacies of self-love, which prevent us from looking at things simply, and God will, if he please, acknowledge our efforts as proof of our great love. But we ourselves will know that this proof was given in very ordinary circumstances.

Yet again, this is surely the most certain proof we can give of our love. In extraordinary circumstances we may readily sacrifice ourselves for a stranger, risking, if need be, our own life to save his. But every ordinary day of our life we will devote only to someone who is very dear to us; only for such a one will we tackle the monotonous round of daily duties, without tiring of them or thinking that we do too much in giving every moment of our lives for him; only for such a one will we take the trouble of trying to anticipate all the time his slightest want, so that we may forestall his every wish. Such faithfulness is the surest mark of great love and where love is lacking, faithfulness will last scarcely any time, unless by chance love should grow out of it.

The same thing is true of divine love. Doubtless the heaviest and most deeply felt trials have their place in God's plans for a soul. They may well be—indeed they very often are—the means he employs to set it on the path of greater generosity, to let it see the joy of total giving. But grace sustains the soul that undergoes such trials and borne by grace it not infrequently rises above itself at such times. Then comes the temptation to lapse, to fall back into the many little human gratifications, the thousand petty nothings of life that, in our great hour of trial, seem to lose their meaning for us so that we think we have grown out of them for ever. By their bearing in face of this temptation we recognize both those for whom the great sacrifice is just an incident, and those whom it really does turn away from all things to surrender entirely to God. Those who can keep going in their simple daily work with the same generosity that grace raised them to in their hour of trial are the ones whom God will know for his own, the ones who will really enter into the mystery of his love.

Faithfulness in little things is the most authentic mark of love, just as it is the surest way of rendering love more pure and more profound, with greater depths of self forgetfulness and humility.

That is why it is not an easy thing; it calls for great generosity; this must spring from an ardent desire which is a gift of grace, given by God to the soul that he wants entirely for himself. He fills the soul with this fervent, persistent desire which will be its strength, its surest support, its firmest prop in the struggle that is to come. Whatever the obstacles, the difficulties to be overcome, it can no longer grow discouraged or give up the task it has begun. The treasure of which it has caught sight is too great to be forgotten; without it nothing remains —neither rest, nor peace, nor happiness—for the soul.

A longing like this is the greatest of all graces, the strongest guarantee against discouragement, the surest pledge of perseverance.

Souls which progress are those which, beset by difficulties and weaknesses of which they are well aware and grieve that they cannot overcome, are yet filled with a great longing that, without let, spurs them to greater effort and will not permit them to give up.

The Prayer of Trust

Such desire is a gift of grace; it is therefore necessary in the first place to be filled with great faith in this grace which sustains our every step, which will never tire, being all merciful.

Faith like this is not always easy to attain; at times, caught up in our all too human feelings, we can too easily come to doubt the reality of this power that is so very well concealed within us. Yet we must not let the fierce flames of human passions eclipse that tiny candle whose single light will one day shine more brightly than they; but even now, when its feeble light is scarce perceptible, we must turn towards it.

Let us take an example. Some anxiety disturbs us unreasonably; it seems impossible to still it without a great deal more detachment and self-surrender. Caught in this agitation, the mind is no longer free; our duties suffer, prayer becomes increasingly difficult, God seems remote. Should we therefore think that we have lost the desire to come only to him, just because we are so deeply caught up in cares that have nothing to do with him and that must be overcome before we dare again lift our eyes to him? That would be to wear ourselves out in vain, in an undertaking doomed to failure from the outset! No matter how faint the still flickering light of our good intention, even though it seem all but smothered by our unrest, yet we must turn to it. This may only be a weak, timid gesture in its direction, that we feel will never be able to overcome our headstrong, vital feelings. Yet it is enough for grace to work upon; it is something for grace to hold on to and give life to. To make an act of good will, simply, like this—without waiting until we can positively feel it to be stronger than the things that are fighting against it—is to open ourselves to the divine influence of grace; grace will answer our call, will perhaps lead us to some slight act of renunciation to give proof of our good will, and that will suffice to bring us a little peace and consolation; and already we will see ourselves more clearly as we are.

So when we don't seem to be making any progress we must not be frightened of trying in our prayers to express feelings that we dare not believe sincere, since we have such great difficulty in putting them into practice. For that is one gateway for grace to enter—narrow, perhaps, but real. God does not disregard evidence of good will, no matter how slight. Rather it seems that once he catches sight of it he can see nothing else, he grasps it as one way of gaining entry into the soul and coming to its aid; and perhaps at length, sustained in this way, the soul will find that the obstacle that seemed so insurmountable at first is really very trivial, and will marvel that it was such a simple matter to overcome it.

Very often, too, there is a great deal that is artificial in these strong attachments that are seemingly so difficult to break off. This becomes apparent when one of them loses its hold over us. Then we wonder how we could have attached such great importance to something that from now on holds no interest for us at all. Or again, how we smile at the agonies others suffer over things that they take greatly to heart but that leave us quite cold. How hollow that attachment seems to us. Yet surely the same could often be said about things that cause us a bitter struggle. For instance, we may be strongly caught in the grips of a feeling of impatience that is gone the moment something else catches our attention. Then we are set free and can stop the mind wandering back to the source of irritation, and prevent ourselves being caught again by that fever from which there will be no escape, once the feelings it arouses in us begin to colour everything for us.

The best way to overcome these emotional upheavals is to distract our attention from them, and gently to turn it towards God. That at least is something we can always do—pray, tell God how much we want to do better, confide our desire to him. But what if our prayer is not accompanied by a generous effort, if it rises from the midst of a thousand lapses, a thousand trials of our weakness which only show up our good intentions as faltering impulses towards God? That is no excuse to give up praying; if prayer is the only thing we are strong enough to offer God, then at least let us offer him that. It is an attempt to stay close by him, who is the source of all holiness and all strength; it is one way of fostering good intentions that will gradually grow in strength, one way of seeing ourselves in proper perspective, simply as we are, screened from the delusions of our self love.

We are glad to turn to the authority of St Teresa of Avila on this point; we can believe what she, the saint of love, of great ecstasies and generous fervour, tells us about the prize that is won by this humble faithfulness in prayer:

> It is not without reason that I have dwelt upon this period of my life at such length . . . (but to show) what great blessings God grants to a soul when He prepares it to live the practice of prayer, though it may not be as well prepared already as it should be; and now, if that soul perseveres, notwithstanding the sins, temptations and falls of a thousand kinds into which the devil leads it, the Lord, I am certain, will bring it to the harbour of salvation. . . . I can say what I know by experience—namely, that no one who has begun this practice, however many sins he may com-

> mit, should ever forsake it. For it is the means by which we may amend our lives again, and without it amendment will be very much harder.
>
> (1, *Life,* ch. 8, pp. 48-50.)

And she returns insistently to this point:

> I only wish I were a person of great authority so that my words might be believed: I beseech the Lord that His Majesty may be pleased to grant me this. I repeat that no one who has begun to practise prayer should be discouraged and say: 'If I am going to fall again, it will be better for me not to go on practising prayer.' I think it will be worse if such a person gives up prayer and does not amend his evil life; but if he does not give it up, he may have confidence that prayer will bring him into the haven of light. . . . He who never ceases walking and advances all the time, may reach his goal late, but does reach it all the same. To lose one's way seems to be the same thing as giving up prayer.
>
> (*Ibid.* ch. 19, pp. 113, 117).

What is more it is by maintaining in this way a constant effort in God's direction that prayer itself grows better and becomes a habitual attitude that prompts everything we do; if it is not constantly recharged by contact with sacrifice, it will gradually wither away. It will not become a way of life, continuously reshaping itself, unless it leads to acts of renunciation which call down graces of light that open new prospects for it.

By these acts the soul will come to a better understanding of its habitual attitude before God; this understanding will tend to be general and confused, but will be a necessary source of strength when the soul is faced with a particular difficulty that must be overcome. And this will be the sign by which we may recognize whether prayer is a real and vital thing in our life. The hour of prayer is occasionally the time when alien thoughts take possession of us most strongly; how are we to know to what extent they really have distracted us from God's presence, which is often hidden and very difficult to discern? While we are actually praying, we cannot form a true opinion of the effects of our prayer; these can more readily be seen by their influence on the whole of our life. Is our life normally lived in a different atmosphere than it would be if we neglected to pray; does concern to be obedient to God's will show itself in everything we do? If so, then our prayer is genuine. But if on the other hand we feel that we have rather lost touch with these supernatural realities, that we no longer have quite the same faithfulness in our everyday lives; if we find ourselves preoccupied with extraneous cares, living more outside ourselves, then, no matter how fervent the time we give to prayer may seem, we would do well to check what road we are on.

For there is no way of separating prayer and renunciation. They grow strong together, sustaining each other, in patient effort that can persevere only because it is nourished by contact with the grace of God, but which takes concrete form in faithfulness to the daily routine.

Sincerity

One of the most profound aspects of purity of intention is sincerity with oneself. This lies first of all in seeing ourselves as we are, simply and straightforwardly—an attitude of loyalty that probably can only be described by setting it in the perspective of our love for our neighbour and showing it as a prime condition of the generous practice of this virtue which, moreover, offers the best opportunities for exercising such self knowledge.

But sincerity lies, too, in being able to recognize the demands of grace with a simple and pure heart, without arousing any return of self interest. It is very necessary to be alert in hearing God's voice and understanding what it means, when he is asking something of us. For the demands God makes of us are the condition without which the plans of his mercy could not be achieved. The heavier his demands, the more precious the gift he is keeping in reserve, and to bypass his wishes by more or less wilfully closing our ears and refusing to hear, out of fear that we might have to respond, is to bypass the graces that God intends for us.

To come freely to God, without let or hindrance.... Surely the greatest suffering of the interior life is to know ourselves restricted by so many things to which we are still so much attached that we cannot think how we could bear to live without them. Yet it is not impossible to give them up, with God's grace and a really great effort. Are we capable of making the effort? It seems as if these exciting, powerful attractions will always be there and very much alive. If only it were a question of open battle with them! But nature is so resourceful, full of such subtle ruses; it puts forward such excellent reasons for granting at least a little of what it asks, for not making just the one sacrifice which may perhaps be essential for our next step forward.

The most difficult part of any renunciation that will cost us too much is honestly to accept the fact that it is asked of us. And when grace, striving to detach us from ourselves, has finally managed to open our eyes, has brought us to acknowledge some fault, some matter that must be rectified in us, surely this is the sign that its work is nearly done, that already the resistance that opposed it has yielded and almost the only thing left to be done is to clear away the rubbish left by the collapse of the obstacle.

To advance in this way in honesty with oneself is to approach the perfect inner liberty of which this is the first condition. Such liberty does not presuppose a firm resolution to fight against the many allurements that seek to enchain the will; it is possible only in so far as these allurements have themselves been sufficiently mortified and have lost enough of their strength no longer to cloud our judgment. That is why we are not necessarily to blame when we are unable to see our way clearly; it could be that the will is in real conflict, struggling to the best of its ability with some attachment, which is still strong enough to disturb our clarity of insight. As St John of the Cross says:

> Although there be no malice conceived in the understanding of the soul, concupiscence and rejoicing in the creature suffice of themselves to create in the soul the first degree of this evil, which is the blunting of the mind and the darkening of the judgment, by which the truth is understood and each thing honestly judged as it is.
>
> (*Ascent of Mt. Carmel,* III, p. 19.)

So we have no cause for surprise at these periods of darkness, this lack of perfect inward clarity. Of course, we must try to arrive at real honesty with ourselves in the end, but this, like the liberty of which it is a condition, can only result from self-conquest. Besides, surely the acceptance of whatever circumstance God has given us, through which he wishes us to make our way towards him, is one aspect of this very honesty with ourselves.

We must honestly admit, therefore, that we are still moved by very lively human feelings and that we are not wholly dominated by love of God. We must be still imperfect when our difficulties still disturb us, when we still suffer from our setbacks; but then, we are imperfect. To want to pretend to ourselves that we are not easily upset would be artificial and false. Let us be much more simple, recognizing that we cannot prevent ourselves from feeling melancholy; we must not try to escape these feelings but submit to them quietly and patiently, letting the fire whose heat we feel do its work, since we know that it is gradually burning away the obstacles to grace that lie in us, those self-attachments that cannot be weakened in any other way.

Of course another, more perfect attitude does exist. It would be better not to feel the humiliation so greatly, to stifle these feelings of impatience more quickly and to turn a more cheerful face towards the persons that we find inwardly irritating, not to be so much disturbed by such slight troubles . . . but we have not yet reached that stage. We must keep trying and not be concerned at having not succeeded so far, not think that God finds this a fault in us. For if we do not, how shall we ever show him a face that is not irritated and then, how shall we ever grow in his love?

God does not judge us in this way; what he looks for is a real effort to make progress towards him. To him faults springing from weaknesses or lack of preparation, our imperfectly controlled emotions, our deficiencies, are like the shavings the carpenter lets fall without noticing, so intent is he on the carving itself.

These scarce mortified failings force us into a struggle which reveals the strength of our love, and that is the only thing that counts in his eyes.

So we must not think the struggle without merit until there is nothing left to fight, the sacrifice without avail until we are so detached that we no longer feel the cost of it.

What is more, these difficulties and obstacles that we still have not been able to overcome do not necessarily mean that our love is any the less strong. It is not possible, of course, for love to grow stronger without robbing the forces that stand in its way of their power. Nonetheless it does happen that one soul, even though it is the more generous, will yet lapse more often than another. It makes many more attempts—which is what God sees—but it encounters many more setbacks. Because of its temperament or its particular circumstances, the problem that faces it is much more difficult to solve. We are not all given the same task to achieve. The important thing is to be faithful to our lot: whatever the circumstances in which we live, the difficulties that we meet either within ourselves or outside us, we must—through all these things, making use of them all and of the struggles they cause us—turn our life into an honest search for God, in which our love for him will find expression.

Patience

We see therefore that to reform ourselves calls for patience. To want to achieve this reform all at once is to ask for the discouragement of having taken on a task which soon enough seems beyond our strength. Listen to St Teresa of Avila, who was not lacking in fervour, or prone to give up at the first difficulty, speaking of one of her spiritual directors:

> He began with the holy determination to treat me as if I were strong . . . so that I should give no offence of any kind to God . . . and, realizing that he was treating me in spiritual matters as though I were going to become perfect immediately, I saw that I should have to be much more careful. In due course, I realized that I should not improve by using the means which he employed with me, for they were meant for a soul which was much more perfect and I, though advanced in divine favours was, as regards virtues and mortification, still quite a beginner. Really, if I had had nobody else to consult, I think my soul would never have shown any improvement, for the distress which it caused me to find that I was not doing what he told me, and felt unable to do so, was sufficient to make me lose hope and give up the whole thing. . . . I say this here, for my whole salvation was due to the fact that

this gentleman knew how to treat me and had the humility and charity necessary for dealing with me and could put up with me when he saw that in some respects I was not amending my life.

(1 *Life*, ch. 23, pp. 148-9.)

Without a doubt, there are certain moments in the spiritual life that mark a definite stage: at such times God calls us more particularly, more insistently, channels our effort into a special direction and gives it new zest. Each of these moments of grace broadens our horizon, opening out wider vistas before us and giving us the strength and support to follow the road ahead. They are like beacons that from time to time light up our way.

But these moments of special privilege only have meaning in the context of the whole work that God is doing in our soul. Out of this context, they will remain somehow unfinished; the gift they bring is a seed whose potentiality can only come to full flower by patient, daily effort. So they are a point of departure and at the same time the end of a phase. It is in both these senses that they mark the stages of the spiritual life. They come at the end of the long slow work that preceded them and prepared the ground for them, they acknowledge what has been achieved so far; once we have covered the road that a first grace lit up for us, a new call from God reveals beyond the stage we have attained, further, higher goals, as yet unsuspected, towards which we must make our way.

Thus one instant of intimate contact with God in prayer will not only bring an increase of courage but will open up new horizons where everything seems simpler, clearer, easier. We will be more keenly aware of God's goodness, of his infinite mercy towards us, and this will increase in us the desire to show towards our neighbour the same lenient goodness; this desire may perhaps be strong enough to keep us, at least for some time, out of the reach of any temptation to impatience. Our relations with others will assume a new meaning and the practice of charity will become natural to us.

We will hear the call of grace also when we must make a particularly deeply felt sacrifice, one that teaches us just what renunciation means; for it will be quite obvious that courage for such a sacrifice can be found only in the consolation and joy that comes from absolute, unreserved giving; everything must be clear cut, we must make up our minds finally to be done with some attachment or other to which we have been clinging; and, in doing so, we will in some way find support in the very compulsion that has driven us to make the choice.

At such times, when in one way or another the support of grace is most felt, everything becomes easy or, at least, we seem to be animated by a new strength. But this feeling does not correspond to the real state in which we are living; it is greatly superior to it. This is proved by the fact that once this time of special fervour is passed we are faced again with our habitual difficulties. But it is not therefore any the less encouraging, since it helps us better to understand the perfection we must aim at, and how far from our reach it is.

The call to a more generous effort can make itself felt in a more austere and humble manner when a humiliating lapse on our part or a good example set by someone else makes us feel more strongly how far we are from the virtue we see in others—much further, perhaps, than we had thought. In this way, too, God renews in us the desire to come to him and a firmer resolve to overcome the obstacles in the way, which we now see more clearly.

But sometimes we do not have a very clear idea of how we have responded to these advances of grace for, when God demands a sacrifice, he does not help us to bear it in the same way every time. Left more to ourselves, we might feel that we had accepted the trial very badly; we might probably be especially aware of how violently we had felt the shock, how strong our self attachment had proved to be. This may simply be because we were involved at a point where there had not previously been any real opportunities for renunciation, and so God's love had come up against an entirely new obstruction that could not be demolished all at once. But God does not ask that of us; all is by no means finished, but this sacrifice, whether well or ill received, has all the same begun the work of demolition; it has served as the instrument of progress; for this reason were we made to encounter it, since it was the one sacrifice that we were capable of at that particular time.

In whatever way these calls of grace make themselves heard, they merely widen the road that lies ahead and it is left to us to achieve by humble faithfulness in our daily tasks the goal we have been allowed to glimpse.

The important thing is to keep going, to persevere

along the humdrum path of our everyday life without being depressed at not seeing clearly just what progress we are really making, nor surprised at encounterng anew the same difficulties, nor giving in to weariness in face of the effort that we must make again and again, without cease, though it seems of no avail. What is important is not to give up struggling and abandon everything because of the seeming impossibility of breaking those attachments that seem too strong for us, of calming the ever-recurrent tempests. In the long run, such persistence will bear fruit. How often, after a long period when, overwhelmed by the burden of our failings, we think we are doing nothing well, does it become apparent that far from having fallen back, we have in fact made some progress. Grace has carried on its work in our heart in secret, all the better perhaps for the depth of our feelings of impotence. For in this work of God so many things are hidden from us; a concealed influence is at work in our soul, transforming it little by little.

That is why, however clumsy our efforts, they sometimes lead to results that astonish us. Quite obviously they have not achieved these things by their own power alone. They have merely provided the opportunity for grace to operate and what this patient, lowly, humble, silent work of grace has accomplished is firm and lasting and we will always possess it—it has brought the soul to a more perfect state of detachment.

We must love this simple, hidden grace, leave it to carry out its work in the depths of our heart, be amenable to it and prompt to remove the obstacles it finds in us.

If we are really convinced that grace is at work in us, how can we still marvel at what in its mercy it can achieve, despite all our weaknesses and failings? These we must learn to tolerate patiently, with that patience towards our own weaknesses which must precede patience towards others, for both are attitudes born of humility.

If we understand that the way of humility is the way of grace, how can we help loving it? The way is lowly, no doubt, but it is also perfect, even if its perfection does not fulfil our human expectations. There is no better proof of constant, faithful love than this persistent, hidden effort that is wearied and discouraged by nothing. Nor is there any more effective way of making our love more pure than by bringing it to those depths where alone humility can be found—humility, that makes our hearts poor, truly empty, that penetrates to the most hidden roots of our self attachments, in order to kill them.

To offer our poverty is not a second-rate offering, for this is the one essential gift—the gift of self or, rather, the gift of all we have to give.

CHAPTER II

Renunciation and trust

Submission

GRACE is patient, it knows how to wait; gradually it makes its way towards its goal, the perfect unity of the completely submissive soul with God. Before we lay claim to this unity we must start by stressing the duality that lies in us, learn to control our will in face of the ever lively impulses of nature, school it every day in a firmer adherence to God. When it is solidly established in this adherence and possesses, as well, God's love which leaves no corner empty and unoccupied, no part of it prone to any other desire, any other joy, then at long last the soul will be beyond the reach of sensual influences. These influences will not only be unable to get at the soul but, cut off from it, the source of their vigour and former strength and vitality, they will gradually wilt even though they may never quite die.

This genuine peace can come only when love holds complete sway over the will, when the will's only desire is to leave God free to do his work in it.

The only way to rid ourselves entirely of those many

imperfections that mar every single thing we do on our own is to let God act in our stead, let him will for us, so that our one desire is to live by his will, to be submissive to everything he wants, accept everything from his hands, as a gift of his kindness.

For that we must come to realize just how flimsy and vain a thing is our will when it stands by itself, just how inconsistent and lacking in depth our desires, when they are simply our own; then we shall not cling to them any more, but let them go as things of no value. What weight can they carry in face of the will of God, whose fullness overwhelms us? If only we could glimpse something of that fullness, and feel how frail and inconsistent, how shallow are our own desires, except in so far as our will is united with God's to make one with it! Then our sole longing would be to make one with him, to do nothing more than consent and cling to him.

Only grace can bring us into the depths of God's will in this way, revealing to us how utterly his will is love, how far the acceptance of his will is primarily an act of faith in this love; an act the more worthy since the circumstances in which we make it almost always ask for renunciation but, above all, for an act of love and of trust. To let ourselves be led by the divine will is to acknowledge therein God's love for us, for us personally; it is to set out joyfully along the way he has chosen, by which he wants to bring us to intimate, personal friendship with him. Such is the height, the depth, the breadth of his love which embraces us all, but at the same time gives itself to each one of us in real intimacy.

The value of a life lies not in having obeyed God's will in this incident or that, but in our manner of accepting it—in whether, by an act of faith and complete trust, we really have seen it as our only good, as a gift of love, no matter under what appearances it came to us. It lies in a trust which is shaken by nothing, in a soul that God can lead by any road he pleases, knowing that it will never cease to believe in his goodness.

This absolute trust is love's pinnacle. It is the most precious feeling there can be in the depths of a loving heart. This is the feeling that we have the greatest joy in finding in those whom we love. Perhaps we never have really seen it in all its purity, except in the eyes of a child. It flourishes only in the heart's humility.

Of course, a soul established in this attitude of child-like trust will not automatically be sheltered from every difficulty and many conflicting emotions, that it can never altogether stifle, will abound in it. But in its depths there will be a source of peace to which it need only turn for these all too human emotions to be, if not entirely stifled, then at least robbed of bitterness and disturbing restlessness.

Yet we will never be allowed to forget the lowliness of our state or the fact that grace shows its power in us, only through our weakness. St Teresa, speaking of the heights of the spiritual life, said thus:

> You must not take it sisters, that the effects which I have described as occurring in these souls are invariably present all the time; it is for this reason that, whenever I have remembered to do so, I have referred to them as being present 'habitually'. Sometimes, Our

Lord leaves such souls to their own nature. . . . Our Lord's will is for the soul not to forget what it is—for one reason, so that it may always be humble. . . . Do not, of course, for one moment imagine that, because these souls have such vehement desires and are so determined not to commit a single imperfection for anything in the world, they do not in fact commit many imperfections and even sins.

(II *Interior Castle,* 7th Mansion, ch. 4, p. 344.)

And elsewhere, she says:

To come back to the question of union. I consider that this is the state of the pure spirit, raised above all the things of the earth, in whom no desire remains that would draw it away from the will of God, but whose mind and will are so much one with God's, detached from all things for him, that it no longer has the slightest vestige of self-love or love of created things. . . . A soul that is always of this generous disposition will walk in the way of right, will make progress, earn merit, but yet one cannot say that it is united to God as in contemplation . . . for the dust of our poor nature, of our faults, and the hindrances with which we furnish ourselves, are so prolific that it is not possible to live with the same purity as the soul united with God, for this is outside and surpassing our wretched state.

(5th *Spiritual Relation.*)

All human perfection is in someway unfinished, imperfect. It is possible that the will can rise to a sincere desire to give itself unrestrainedly and this really will be what it wants, so long as it is alone before God, in prayer. But when it is once again involved in the mutability of daily life, subject to all those influences that are at work on it, always prone to stir up some new desire, how can it maintain perfect calm in a sovereign place that nothing can assail? How can it always be as clear then as it is in prayer? As St Teresa has told us, such unshakeable firmness is beyond the reach of our wretched nature. We cannot aspire to so great a triumph. We will always have to struggle. Does this mean that the enemy will never be completely vanquished? We are not asked to achieve outright victory, but only to show by the fervour with which we fight, how truly we desire the good the foe seeks to destroy. The prize that our efforts are to win is not perfection without strain. Nor is it a completely human perfection: we are not called upon to bring to perfection some wonderful type of humanity. In this plan, which is not of his choosing, God is pleased to leave blanks and inferiorities in the soul that he wants for himself. He shows it how poor, clumsy even, it will always be on this earth, its natural country, which belongs to its nature; and so he reminds it that the ways of his love are not the same as those in which our pride loses its way, the goal his love has in view is not that in which our pride takes comfort. In this way he makes the soul see how greatly the perfection he offers it differs from that which it can possess as its natural good. This is a very great truth which, being a mystery of love, is also a mystery of humility.

Surrender

Humility is the condition of love. Only humility makes

possible love's crowning testimony, the unreserved gift of self that finds expression in trust: surrender. Surrender is the attitude of a soul that has nothing left of its own, and knows how truly the things it loves, the only things that have any interest for it, are things of God, belong to him only and so must be left in his charge for him to dispose of as he pleases.

To trust in Providence does not mean to rely on Providence to carry out our own plans, but rather to have no plans of our own; none, at least, that we are not ready to renounce so that God may achieve his own purposes. For his ways are not our ways. Our ways, to which we hold so tenaciously, will seem like changing dreams, mists blown by the wind, our lost hopes will soon be forgotten when we see where God, leading us by a path not of our own choice, has taken us.

There will be nothing left to regret, nothing in us will be unfulfilled, when we see the more perfect gift that God has been keeping for us. For through our complete adherence to his will we will come to live in a world of greater truth and deeper reality than this world where our desires lead us astray and we will discover, far surpassing everything we have had to give up to follow him, the things to which he alone can bring us, the only things that can satisfy our heart.

It is not things that we must renounce, but simply the desire for things as things. What will drop away and be effectively abandoned is what is worthless and inconsistent in the objects of our desires. What has true value in them will be found in God's will and, in fact, can only be found there. For it is in God's will that all things assume their value and meaning and are seen in their true light.

That is the real meaning of renunciation. It is not a matter of being cut off, having nothing more to do with our surroundings, but of looking at everything with new eyes, in a different perspective. Seen thus, every circumstance of our life becomes an occasion of 'uniting ourselves with God in hope', as St John of the Cross so beautifully puts it. For union with God who is all love, is expressed in an act of faith and hope, in the entire trust of a soul who has put itself in God's hands and lets him dispose of it as he wishes, since it belongs to him. His will be done; *his will,* just because it is his, and is all love.

It is not so much a matter of not doing anything, of passivity; but of acting in a different way, of putting God's activity before our own; this will mean counting less on our own efforts, our own foresight and human calculations and giving more room to trust and submission. This will show itself in a thousand ways.

First of all, we will lose all anxiety in the pursuit of even the best of our desires, we must not want to reach any goal by relying on methods of our own choice, which it seems to us must be the best. On the contrary, we will proceed in simplicity and freedom of spirit with the task we feel ourselves obliged to perform, without worrying about impediments, or troubling over difficulties as if everything depended on ourselves and we had to succeed. In this way we will find it easier to give up some way of going about things which may have seemed useful and even legitimate but which it would be better not to use since, for example, it might give offence to someone who has a grudge towards us but nonetheless deserves to be treated with kindness and consideration inspired by true charity. We choose not to make use of a human means, even though it seems to lead to the end in view, and to stay closer to God, leaving things more to his direction.

We simply try to become part of the providential course of events, to support its accomplishment as best we may, by doing what we can in the circumstances that offer themselves to us, and by knowing how to wait, how to be patient, without seeing immediate results for our efforts. The more nearly an action is done in this spirit of humble goodwill and self-surrender, the more naturally and unforcedly it will fit into the design of providence. It is by renouncing like this any independent action that we do most to further the fulfilment of God's plan, which he alone can know.

To stick to a purely human outlook, to try to lead one's life by one's own skill, relying on oneself, is to run the risk of losing courage when setbacks and difficulties occur; but to give oneself into God's hands is to be assured of dwelling there in peace. He will lead us into the unknown; we have only to follow him, taking care all the time to go at the pace he asks of us—that is, to try to discern how to act in every circumstance, what attitude to adopt in order to show, in the simplest and most perfect way, our pure desire for complete obedience. Then obstacles and set-backs will count for little. They will come into the same category as success and will serve an even better purpose than success can do—for our part, they will serve to keep us in a state of humble submission and from God's point of view, they may perhaps be a way of diverting us from a blind alley that we have entered in all good faith and turning us again in the right direction. When our human plans meet a check, the divine purpose is working itself out in a different way. Or again, sometimes God, before granting us some good he intends us to have, simply wants to try our faith by seeming to remove our desire from our reach and thereby to purify any imperfect attachment we may have for it, any quite natural feelings which may unwittingly be mixed with our good desire and confused by us with it.

It is by making ourselves completely docile and amenable to Providence's guidance in this way that we can be sure that we really are in his hands, that his activity, freely and unhampered at work in us, can reveal its complete effectiveness. Many things, that human means confess themselves impotent to deal with, will be resolved; and this will point to the influence of a solicitous and benevolent will. We must admit, for instance, that in some matter that has not turned out as we wanted, a better solution was reached, whereby a more far-sighted purpose than ours was served. Or again we can say that in choosing the path we did at some crucial moment in our lives, we could not have foreseen all the consequences that were to flow from that decision, nor perhaps could we have guessed the real reasons why it was the best choice for us. Surely God, by means of the choice we make from different motives, leads us where he wants us to go.

The truest and most profound form that self renunciation takes is surrender to the will of God. To have no will apart from his, to leave him to carry out his purposes, caring for nothing but to be amenable to them—that is how to make our lives the expression of our love for God, of our trusting love in which this joy of being entirely given to him, in an unreserved gift of self, blends with the joy of acknowledging with thanksgiving how good it is to abide in his hands: 'That which my Father hath given me is greater than all; and no one can snatch them out of the hand of my Father' (John 10, xxix).

Love's Fulfilment

CHAPTER I

Union with God

A Union of simplicity and purity

PRAYER is the summit of the Christian life. Everything leads towards it, for in prayer takes place our meeting with God, towards which all our efforts tend.

The best way to understand prayer is to consider it under its most perfect forms where it is truly, in all its fullness, itself. Indeed we cannot form an altogether just idea of prayer if we limit ourselves to a consideration of its most elementary forms. To discern what is only obscurely foreshadowed in elementary prayer, it must be viewed in the light of what we learn from the purest forms of prayer; it is in these pure forms moreover, that the most essential characteristics of prayer, where we gain a truer knowledge and a greater love of it, are most surely established.

So it is not by any means vain curiosity or ambitious presumption to turn to these forms of prayer that people call 'higher'—it would surely be better to call them 'more profound', thereby implying at the outset not that they carry the aura of some sort of sublimity inducive of pride but that, from the depths of inner nakedness wrought by humility and renunciation, they bring a closer contact with God.

Let us for the moment limit ourselves to considering prayer as it appears to us in its first stages. What idea can we form of it? At first it seems essentially an effort of thought, of reflection; to pray, we think of God. So the important thing seems to be to hit upon considerations that are capable of striking us sufficiently, to keep the mind alert and arouse in the heart a feeling of love, love which will gain in fervour to the extent that our meditation has been able to penetrate into the mystery that has been before it.

This effort of concentration will grow easier with practice; we will learn how to prolong it with greater facility and in a simpler way. Moreover it is unlikely that grace will not from time to time nourish it and let it make more intimate contact with God. In such rare moments the soul will not fail to realize that the essential thing about prayer lies not in what the soul can achieve by itself but in a pure gift from God, that he grants when it pleases him. Nonetheless, in actual fact prayer of this kind does seem to the soul to be primarily the fruit of its own efforts. To the extent that it can maintain an attitude of recollection, keeping to thoughts bent on God, singling out for contemplation some aspect that can move the heart and arouse a greater longing for him who is its only good, the soul will grow in love and be more deeply rooted in it.

Come a period of dryness, and the soul will no doubt try to console itself with the thought that God will take pity on it when it has done all that lies in its own power, yet will find it hard not to grow anxious, not to think that it is losing time, that its prayer is of no avail, since it cannot carry on in the way that seemed so beneficial to it, by which it was able to draw such tangible profit from the hours of prayer. Such moments of aridity must seem to the soul to obstruct its passage, to be a temporary trial which must be endured as well as can be but after which, or so at least it hopes, it will come to a more fervent prayer by means of which it will go on gradually enriching itself in a more perfect knowledge of the mysteries of God, which are the constantly renewed source of more ardent love. Such is the path we expect to tread, using this effort of attention to God as a means of infusing everything we do with a more genuinely spiritual intention, making a place in our life for prayer, of course, even a place of esteem, but not of such esteem that we make it the summit towards which everything converges.

And should we hope to make some progress along this path, and think that some day grace may open new vistas before us, we readily picture these as being the same sort of thing, as it were a sublimation of the effort by which we seek to arouse in the soul, by means of thoughts that fix the mind on him, feelings of love for God. This effort to meditate, we presume, will take on a different tempo, our understanding will be illuminated by such strong light on the divine mysteries that love will burst into flames of ardour hitherto unknown.

We are set on an altogether different path by the teaching of St John of the Cross and the truth he lets us see is far more profound. For him, the true way to reach intimate union with God is not by ever enriching our prayer with increasingly heightened insights into God's infinite majesty but, on the contrary, constantly to deepen our awareness of our utter poverty in his sight. As usual, he expresses this by quoting from Scripture:

> ... We shall quote that passage of David, wherein he clearly described the great power which is in this might for bringing the soul this lofty knowledge of God. He says, then, thus: In the desert land, waterless, dry and pathless, I appeared before Thee, that I might see Thy virtue and Thy glory. It is a wondrous thing that David should say here that the means and the preparation for his knowledge of the glory of God were not the spiritual delights and the many pleasures which he had experienced, but the aridities and detachment of his sensual nature, which is here understood by the dry and desert land.
>
> (*Night,* bk. 1, ch. 13, p. 388.)

The essence of prayer, the most profound thing about it, has therefore nothing to do with sublime notions and grand illuminations by which the soul is raised to an exalted idea of spiritual realities. The purest and most fruitful graces do not belong to these various species of 'vision and revelations' of which St John of the Cross says that these are never anything but 'curtains and veils to cover the spiritual' (*Ascent of Mount Carmel* bk. II, ch. 16). What is gained in that manner are only 'little bits of spiritual communication' by which the soul 'grows used to spiritual things' (*ibid.,* ch. 17). But to reach 'the substance of the spirit' a more austere way must be followed, and the soul must dwell 'in poverty and spiritual nakedness' (*ibid.,* ch. 15) 'detached, stripped bare, pure and simple' (*ibid.,* ch. 16), to open itself to a more hidden, more secret grace that John of the Cross calls faith, pure, living faith.

'Faith, the wondrous means, which leads to the goal, which is God' (*Ascent,* bk. II, ch. 2, p. 68). We can compare it to the torches held by the soldiers of Gideon 'which they saw not, because they had them concealed in the dark pitchers; and, when these pitchers were broken, the light was seen. Just so does faith, which is foreshadowed by these pitchers, contain within itself divine light; which when it is ended and broken, at the ending and breaking of this mortal life, will allow the glory and light of the Divinity which was contained in it, to appear'. (*ibid,* ch. 9, p. 99-100.) Completely hidden though it may be, this light is already present in faith; in faith the soul finds its God, is united with him; by faith it adheres to him, just as it is him that it will behold in the beatific vision. 'The only difference is that we will see God, where now we believe in him', but it is really he whom we attain, and the spirit 'established in faith' will remain 'interiorly at rest, at peace' (*ibid.,* ch. 8). St John of the Cross never wearies of repeating how 'by means of this loving and hidden knowledge God unites himself with the soul to an exalted and divine degree; for in some way this loving and hidden knowledge which is faith serves in this life for the divine union just as in heaven the light of glory serves for clear vision of him' (*ibid,* ch. 22).

'This hidden and loving knowledge which is faith.' In what way can faith be said to be 'knowledge'? To understand this we must try to grasp the meaning of the two qualifications St John of the Cross attributes to it—'loving' and 'obscure'. He goes so far as to say 'purgation, contemplation, or poverty of spirit . . . these are all almost one and the same thing (*Night,* bk. II, ch. 4, p. 404). It is hidden for two reasons: first because the soul itself is full of imperfections, faults, shadows, which are beyond its understanding. That is why the work of grace is at first purifying and painful; just as 'material fire, acting upon wood, first of all begins to dry it . . . then it begins to make it black, dark and unsightly . . . and, finally, it begins to kindle it externally . . . and at last transforms it into itself and makes it as beautiful as fire' (*Night,* bk. II, ch. 10, p. 429); in the same way when the light of grace starts to shine 'into the extreme gloom of the dark places of the soul, the soul sees its natural and vicious shadows which are a hindrance to spiritual light . . . until, when this divine light has managed to disperse these shadows, the soul is enlightened and sees itself transformed into light'. Even then, moreover, this divine light is absolutely pure ' . . . not only in the darkness and afflictions of purgation, when this wisdom of love purges the soul, and the soul is unable to speak of it, but equally so after an illumination, when this wisdom is communicated to it most clearly. Even then, it is still so secret that the soul cannot speak of it . . . and can find no suitable way or manner to describe . . . such delicate spiritual feeling' (*ibid.,* ch. 17, p. 456). For there is still the second reason why this light remains hidden: 'the heights of divine wisdom which so greatly exceeds the soul's capacity' (*ibid.,* ch. 5). Not only does it remain hidden, but the more perfect it becomes the purer, more simple and unencumbered it grows. 'This general knowledge whereof we are speaking is at times so subtle and delicate, particularly when it is most pure, and simple, and perfect, most spiritual and interior, that although the soul be occupied therein, it can neither realize it nor perceive it' (*Ascent,* bk. II, ch. 14, pp. 121-2). For, the closer God is to us, the more we sense the infinite delicacy of his grace, the image of his infinite purity.

So this is a first lesson we learn from a study of these higher stages of prayer or, as John of the Cross calls them, the 'more inward' stages. We see, clearly apparent, one of the essential qualities of prayer—it is and it must be simple, unencumbered.

But whence comes this purity, this lack of encumbrance, essential for really profound prayer? John of the Cross recurs to this point ceaselessly and we could quote a thousand passages on the subject: the soul must renounce everything in itself from which it might draw support—'this spiritual light . . . so simple, so pure and so general holds all the faculties of the soul empty and devoid of all its understanding'; the soul must come to recognize its impotence, its nothingness, it must accept the path 'of poverty and surrender' so that gradually it will be able to come to 'its centre of humility'. For it is 'in humanity' that the soul will attain 'the purity, the sensitivity through which it may become one with the spirit of God'.

St. Thérèse of the Child Jesus' translation of this 'pure faith' of John of the Cross into her conception of surrender was therefore quite natural.

Now we see what is the link between the 'hidden' and the 'loving' knowledge of faith; for in this very concealment love grows deeper—the soul, recognizing that it can do nothing on its own, learns to surrender itself to the care of him for whom everything is possible; by recognizing that everything it has comes from him, it learns how truly it belongs to him alone. It glimpses how deeply, with what utter submission, this absolute belonging, which penetrates every fibre of its being, must be expressed. It knows that it is completely possessed.

Then does it truly live in faith, in this pure and living faith which is an act of absolute trust in God; the more complete our awareness of our own nothingness, the more profound will our trust be. When we are completely stripped of ourselves and our faith springs from a genuine awareness of our poverty, then it really is the response of a soul who has nothing left of its own, is completely free, completely at the disposal of love, who may do with it what he will, for it desires nothing but to rest in his hands.

And, in this act of trust, through which it comes to meet the infinite gratuitousness of love, at the heart of this mystery, the soul feels the presence of him who is its source: the God who is love. It comes to him through that same love by which it lives: faith, that 'hidden and loving knowledge', is wrapped round with divine love which is communicated to it 'in wonderful and sublime knowledge of God' (*Ascent of Mount Carmel* bk. II, ch. 5).

If the 'right and fitting way' to union with God, if the central grace and heart of prayer, is like this, then this should apply to prayer of any degree whatsoever.

Prayer is really prayer to the extent that it is filled with awareness of our nothingness in the sight of God, and it is Christian prayer to the extent that this nothingness is entrusted to love.

Everything that makes us feel our poverty more

deeply, that increases in us the nakedness of humility, will help us approach God with greater certainty. We will find him at the heart of this poverty and humility which make us responsive to his love, to the free gift of his love. That is why, far from impeding us, the dryness and the aridity, all those things that make us feel our inability to raise ourselves towards God, have already directed us to a more perfect way of prayer, to the deepest and most essential part of prayer—these, and many other things also, help us along the path of humility: setbacks and trials (for suffering, too, makes us humble), difficulties that prevent us from achieving what we have set our hearts on, anything that makes us aware of our imperfections and limitations; these are the means by which the nakedness of humility is wrought within us. By these means and also, perhaps even more, by faithfulness to the great Christian commandment: 'Love one another'. For this, demanding as it does self-forgetfulness, patience, humility, self-effacement, is the striking way to achieve this progress that is so essential to prayer. We can never stress too much—and here again St Thérèse of Lisieux springs to mind—how intimately linked is progress in prayer with the practical generosity and real forgetfulness of self that charity to one's neighbour demands.

This is what we learn from those who, because they have known the highest reaches of prayer, are best able to tell us what prayer is, what is most essential in it, upon what vital points we should bring our efforts to bear if we want to proceed straight to the goal or, at least, towards it.

There is no more direct way than the 'straight short road' of which St John of the Cross speaks, to reach our goal, which is union with God: it is the way of self deprivation, of renunciation and humility.

'Union with God'—that is the meeting, in this mystery of divine generosity that is love, of the soul who has nothing and the God who gives all he has, because he is Love.

A union of love and grace[1]

Prayer is essentially contact with God; in one way or another, it is always a search for God's presence, for a personal encounter with him.

So prayer cannot be just a mental exercise, not just an effort in concentration and reflection, for the sake of the better discernment of the meaning of a truth that we should like to know more about. It is something more vital and also more tangible, and man's whole vital and tangible being is engaged in it.

So, if we are to understand the real nature of prayer in its essence, it is best first of all to designate various activities that approach prayer very nearly—so nearly in fact that, by creating an atmosphere in which prayer can scarcely be altogether lacking, they can very easily be taken as the same thing, so that we come more or less to confuse the two.

Thus, for example, the study of theology or spiritual reading, begun with the intention of improving our knowledge of the doctrinal grounds of the interior life or its laws of development, are not by themselves prayer; nor are reflection, 'meditation', in which we seek above all to enrich the mind, to gain a better knowledge of a truth, to penetrate the meaning of a mystery. We do not

[1]St John of the Cross.

dispute that such activities lead to prayer, nor even that they lead to it so well that it is difficult to be engaged in them in the right way without more or less praying at the same time. In a reflective atmosphere of this sort, in the presence of these truths filled with God, the soul feels the awakening of impulses which will raise it towards him and bring it into some sort of contact with him. But only this contact, this person to person encounter, is real prayer, and the soul cannot attain it without experiencing the need to seek him out for itself, letting go the means that were able to bring it so far and at last abiding in God's presence alone and in silence.

This does not detract anything from the value of these means without which the goal would not have been reached, but it does advise us not to form an idea of prayer too much in the image and likeness of the ways that lead to it, not to think of it too much as an intellectual exercise, a meditative effort akin to other activities of the mind.

For that would singularly diminish prayer and altogether misinterpret its requirements.

Prayer, as we have said, is a meeting with God, a personal contact with him; it is a person to person encounter in which each opens himself to the other; each truly enters into communion with the other.

The word we use for this is 'loving each other', but it is too easy for those words to conjure up first of all a feeling, an emotion that can go with love but is not itself love. Love comes before all else, it is essentially the free gift of self. It is the idea of *free* giving that reveals its profundity, its infinite purity and delicacy and yet, even with all this richness, its infinite dispossession.

We cannot think of this without realizing what a reform of our selfish, self-enclosed natures, chained down by so many bonds, incapable of freeing ourselves, is demanded by such a turning outwards to another being, whoever he may be, but especially when he is that being who is the apotheosis of giving and generosity, he who is love itself.

So the grace of prayer cannot expand in the soul without gradually working what we may call a remoulding of our whole self; our whole being is involved in prayer; our own most secret, most deep-rooted dispositions will find themselves transformed. Our elemental, impervious self-interest must give way. It hardens everything within us, and without our being aware of it, influences all our judgements and actions, from the most immediate and irrational reaction to our long-deliberated opinions, whose motives we think we fully discern; the only thing we do not know about them is how far they are ordained by this basic orientation which decrees in advance the place and meaning that our self-interest assigns to everything in the scheme of things.

All this must give way to a new attitude, to certain very simple basic dispositions that we will grow to love, which will become ingrained in our soul, the joy and light of our life once we have proved, in prayer, how beneficial they are, freeing us from ourselves and opening us to God; once these dispositions inform everything we do, every judgement we make, our most impulsive reactions, then everything will take on a new colour, will become bright and clear, and we will know ourselves to be set free.

An inner liberation of this kind can only happen as the result of grace penetrating, enlightening and strengthening us. We must of course be responsive to this grace and the first form the responsiveness will take will be to turn our mind towards God. But although our thoughts, 'what we apprehend and have insight with' can be of some help to us in this, yet no matter how lofty they may be they are no more able than 'consolations or spiritual feelings, states of comfort or excitement in God' to be 'the proper, fit means of union with God'. St John of the Cross, whose expressions these are, tells us that none of these things serve as immediate means to union with God.

> For, although these considerations and forms and manners of meditation are necessary to beginners, in order that they may gradually feed and enkindle their souls in love by means of sense (as we shall say hereafter), and although they thus serve them as remote means to union with God, through which a soul has commonly to pass in order to reach the goal and abode of spiritual repose, yet they must merely pass through them, and not remain ever in them . . . the stairs of a staircase have naught to do with the top of it and the rooms to which it leads, yet are means to the reaching of both; and if the climber left not behind the stairs below him until there were no more to climb . . . he would never reach the top of them. (*Ascent*, bk. II, ch. 12, pp. 111-2.)

Does this mean only that such 'beginners' will one day give up the practice of meditation, with the manifold reflections that provide the mind with plentiful and varied food, so that they may yield to a simpler, less embellished but much deeper way of prayer, in which grace is more actively present? Is it enough to advise them to carry on faithfully with this more personal effort of contemplation until 'the time and season to leave it have arrived, and this comes when God brings the soul into a more spiritual communion, which is contemplation' (*Ascent* bk. II, ch. 6, p. 4).

If we did so, we would be contenting ourselves with one single aspect of this progress in prayer, and neglecting another, which throws further light on the primary and most basic requirements of union with God and hence on prayer, by which this union is achieved. As John of the Cross says, we are disposed for this union not by the 'soul's hearing, nor its taste, nor feeling, nor imaginings about God, nor by any thing else at all, but only by purity of love, which is total nakedness and perfect resignation towards God'. (*Ascent,* bk. II, ch. 5.)

Hence, some sort of psychological purification that prepares the mind to apprehend a purer light, to reach God in a simpler act of contemplation, is not enough. The soul must become receptive to the light of love, and it will gradually be able to do so, it will learn to live in this love by virtue of the detachment that this very same love will effect within it, and as, in the course of this action, the requirements of love are revealed, so also will its hidden depths show themselves.

That is the teaching of *The Dark Night of the Soul.* In the prologue to *The Ascent of Mount Carmel,* St John of the Cross had already mentioned the compassion aroused in him by the numbers of souls of goodwill 'who labour and weary themselves to a piteous extent, and yet go backward, seeking profit in that which is not profitable, but is rather a hindrance'.

Therefore he wants to try to help them know 'the road that they ought to follow, if they aspire to the summit of the Mount'. (*Ascent*, Prologue, p. 14.)

What is this initial error that, from the outset, starts us off on the wrong track and which must be put right unless we want to strive in vain? It lies in thinking that the more keenly we relish the things of God, the closer we are to perfection; in taking pleasure in facile prayers that an inward preference bids us prolong; in finding nothing but joy and consolation in the practice of virtue and mortifications, of which our generous soul can never have enough to satisfy its appetite.

All these things have so little substance. They are the tit-bits that God uses to attract a soul still immersed in sensual things, that could not be conquered in any other way.

Once the soul has been attracted in this way, the main work is by no means done . . . far from it! The crucial time will come when God takes away these supports. Then it will be seen whether they were sufficient to root the soul in a deeper love, to bind it so strongly to God that it will remain faithful to him now that it is deprived of them. That is when the future of the soul will be resolved. Until then, nothing decisive has been done.

No doubt God has already conferred on the soul a great grace, one which has opened for it the greatest potentialities, in letting it hear these calls which—in a manner still imperfect but fitted to its weakness and its capability of grasping them—have enabled it to divine those inner realities to which no human means but the grace of God alone can open its eyes. But now the soul must commit itself to these realities more deeply and genuinely. It is still not possible to know whether it truly loves the realities themselves, or just the tangible joys and consolations in which it takes delight, not unmixed with imperfect feelings in which a too self-conscious awareness of being the faithful servant, in whom the Master can find no lack of devotion to reproach, reveals itself in a singular zealousness for justice and an almost excessive readiness to condemn anyone who falls away.

I have no doubt that this love is sincere but there is still a great deal of dross in it, which needs to be purified. A lot remains to be done before it is perfectly pure, detached from everything alien to it. This is the work that grace has now to do in the soul: it must, of course, render the soul's love more fervent but the way to do this is precisely by rendering it more pure, more genuine; the soul's hidden strength must be developed by an increasingly absolute stripping away of everything that might conceal the slightest blemish.

So we can see what a great delusion it is—a delusion that John of the Cross exposes in the prologue to *Mount Carmel*—to think we are losing ground because the love we feel for God, our longing to follow him, do not seem so ardent as formerly they did. There is a further explanation for this delusion: this emotional attraction to serve God with generosity may both supplement and disguise the deficiencies of a will still not firmly anchored to the good. But now these deficiencies show up all too clearly; now we see how weak we still are, torn in every direction by the desires of our poorly-mortified self-love! It becomes so hard to master these desires, which make themselves felt just when the attraction for the things of God fails to uphold us; this attraction is just as much a matter of the emotions and, in a way, is felt on the same level as human attractions and, by the Grace of God, it is stronger than they; we only have to follow where they lead. . . .

Everything seems lost; yet now is the time when everything is beginning, when we are entering on the serious task, wherein decisive progress can be made.

This progress is not achieved by the path of simple enrichment—not by enhanced fervour, nor an ever lively awareness of God's love, whence the soul may refresh itself in prayer that every day is easier and more spontaneous. The way of progress is the way of the Cross: of that mystery of death and resurrection that lasts through the whole Christian life, from which prayer which is its heart and central activity is no escape. It may in the end lead to enrichment, but the way lies through an increasingly utter divestment of self.

So this poor soul, that yesterday was overwhelmed with gifts and virtue, running easily in the path of love, today is weakly and without strength. What has it done to deserve such dereliction? That is the first question we will be tempted to ask and probably we can scarce believe those who say that this is neither penalty nor punishment, neither retreat nor return, but rather the normal way, the first steps towards a more genuine, more profound meeting with God.

What soul, devastated by such dryness and aridity, has not been tempted to look on it all as a defeat, to give up an effort that seems condemned to failure? And yet, if we keep faith, if we can wait, patiently, accepting the humiliation of seeing ourselves poor, powerless, dragging along these lowly ways of difficult prayer, that seems to be so mediocre and earthbound, then from this emptiness and devastation, gradually, probably hiddenly, a deeper, truer grace will make itself felt.

Contrite, humbled, we will learn not to think of ourselves as superior to others but to make allowances for them, in a spirit of sweetness and friendliness that our own wretchedness has taught us. Grown more genuine, more sincere in our poverty and nakedness, we will persevere in our barren labour, not always meeting with success but unfailingly, constantly keeping on, so that at least we are faithful and persevering in looking for God, even though we cannot find him. In this way we will consolidate the profound adherence of our will to this hidden God.

It is this pure attachment of the will to God that makes the soul accessible to the deeper, more hidden workings of grace. Even while we are struggling to persevere faithfully, we may perhaps feel a new emotion, as strong as it is simple and peaceful, growing and taking shape within us—in submitting our will to God's, we will find overwhelming happiness. Something in the depths of the soul makes us choose this attitude of complete docility, so that it seems to our eyes the only good, the source of all peace, all joy, through which we acquire a new strength to make the renunciations that are asked of us. It is a hidden grace, but one in which the soul has the feeling of having for the first time made profound contact with God.

Then we feel that we have everything, there is nothing further to be sought. And yet, we have not come to the end of our efforts nor of our discoveries: the riches of grace are by no means exhausted yet, and they will gradually be revealed.

No doubt it is in one sense true that everything is contained in this union of the will which, John of the Cross tells us, is the whole of union with God (*Mount Carmel,* bk. 11, ch. 5). But there is still much to be done to free the soul from itself absolutely, so that everything within us is subject, and 'gives place absolutely to God' (*ibid*).

The soul will come more and more to look upon this union of the will with God as a mystery into which grace leads us further every day, progressively revealing what it demands of us. It is a mystery: it is not even enough to say that this submission must be so complete as to become the expression of the creature's utter dependance on his Creator. In an even more profound sense, it is the expression of the soul's utter belonging to God, who has taken possession of us by this gift of his grace, making us live with his life, which is love and giving.

This is the submissiveness of love, love which is an image of that life of love which is the life of the Holy Trinity, a participation in the holiness of God himself. The soul sees that it loves God *in* God. It is aware not so much of giving itself to him as of letting itself be possessed by a new life which turns it towards him. Then it has a much better understanding of how surpassing is this mystery which confronts it, into which it has entered only through the absolutely free and condescending gift of God.

So, in this way, through the hidden working of grace, which renders simpler and deeper the will's adherence to God, the soul is brought to the very heart of the mystery of God's love, and of the absolute spontaneity of this love! This spontaneity shines through the very obscurity of grace: the more hidden its activity in the soul, the better the soul's understanding that here is something that does not belong to it, something that it cannot bend to its own whim. Living in this way with a power which is not its own, the soul knows itself as it were dispossessed. It effaces its whole self in humility, submission, thanksgiving. It feels that its entire being is sweetened by a new and very pure joy: the joy of dispossession, of being poor and stripped bare at the hands of him who by his gifts gives it life, of entering into the mystery of spontaneous love.

An even deeper humility than springs from the awareness of our weaknesses and betrayals is that which flows from our knowledge of the absolute freedom of God's gifts. Do our sins humble us? Most certainly, but still more are we humbled by grace—by the quite new manner of realizing how deep is our nothingness in presence of the work that God alone is achieving in us; by coming, in the beautiful words of John of the Cross, through this 'to the heart of our humility', so that we may find there that 'subtle, simple and delicate' purity which enables the soul to 'be one with the spirit of God', to enter into the mystery of his generosity.

John of the Cross teaches us that this purification is achieved by means of a very pure light which the soul cannot experience without seeing its own shortcomings thrown into relief: this light, the light of love, pure with that complete purity that belongs to love, chases the 'shadows and impurities' from the soul, sullied with all the blotches of self-love, rendered dark and coarse by that inward hardness which is the fruit of self-attachment. Now it sees its wretchedness; it feels how far it still is from the infinite clarity and limpidity of grace. But this same humiliation will gradually lead—once again by the way of deprivation which is the way of the cross, making it die unto itself so that it may rise again to a higher life—to the purity of a soul really stripped of itself, a purity that is in some sense itself a gift from God—a soul that is at last brought into the mystery of this love and freedom in which it communes with its God.

It is in this way that the union of will, which the soul had thought to be all that was involved in union with God, grows deeper, is enriched in new ways, in proportion as it draws near to the heart of this mystery of divine generosity, in whose likeness it must be formed.

The soul realizes the truth that it can no longer belong to itself in any way at all; it senses how radical must be the disappropriation of self, without which it is not possible to enter this mystery of freedom—the freedom of giving, of complete generosity—where there is no room for any belonging, to which 'the still possessive soul' of which John of the Cross speaks, may never come.

Truly, the soul no longer belongs to itself, it is once more in the hands of God, delivered to the infinite goodness of his good will; the whole being gives assent to his will and surrenders itself. Only one desire remains: to offer God that supreme testimony of love, an act of absolute trust: the only joy it wants is to be entrusted to him whom it loves, to let him dispose of it as he will; so long as it belongs to him, so long as everything in it abides in his will, his will which is love, it knows that in his love it possesses everything.

We do not make real contact with God through a series of illuminations, each more vivid than the last, that let us 'contemplate' him by an ever purer light—no, it is achieved through the long action of grace in the soul. that works its total transformation, despoiling it, stripping it of every belonging, in order to bring it into this mystery of love, where it is made one with God, who is love.

God is love, and by living with this love we gain some idea of him, and sense that he is present.

Such is the path that leads to God; and perhaps this is the place to ask just how far the term *contemplation,* so traditional and on many counts so exact, runs the risk of causing confusion? Our goal should be *union with God* which in this life, as the whole of Christian tradition is unanimous in teaching, has nothing to do with any heightened knowledge, anything that could be called a 'vision' of God; it means *love.* We cannot live in this love without the sense of God stirring within us; assuredly, this is one way of knowing him, but such a knowledge is the fruit of humble fidelity to grace which is present in us, like the yeast that will cause the whole loaf to rise. Above all, it is important not to forget that fidelity like this requires daily submissiveness to God's will as it shows itself in the circumstances of our lives, humble, trusting submissiveness through which and in which the soul, by living out this mystery of love, comes gradually closer to its hidden centre. And before all else, we must be submissive to the first, supreme commandment, the Law Christ laid down for us: 'Love one another'. Charity towards our neighbour is the place where the grace of prayer joins with our personal effort: it brings within our grasp the means to achieve a more sensitive awareness of the humble self-forgetfulness that we must have to open ourselves to another being; and so it sets us on the road that the grace of prayer will light for us, rendering us, by the dispossession of our selves, increasingly alive to this mystery of God's love, of his spontaneous generosity, into which it wishes to bring us.

The Demands of Love

CHAPTER I

Our Lord's command

In a well-known passage, St Teresa of Avila reminds us that one thing alone matters: conformity with the will of God—for that alone constitutes the necessary condition, or rather the very essence of union with him:

> There is a great deal to be gained by entering this Mansion, and those from whom the Lord withholds such supernatural gifts will do well to feel that they are not without hope; for true union can quite well be achieved, with the favour of Our Lord, if we endeavour to attain it by not following our own will but submitting it to whatever is the will of God. For I tell you, and I shall often repeat this, that when you have obtained this favour from the Lord, you need not strive for that other delectable union which has been described, for the most valuable thing about it is that it proceeds from this union which I am now describing.
> (5th *Mansion*, ch. 3, pp. 259-60.)

But what is this will of God, and what does he expect of us?

> The Lord asks only two things of us: love for His Majesty and love for our neighbour. It is for these

two virtues that we must strive, and if we attain them perfectly, we are doing His will and so shall be united to Him.

(*5th Mansion, ch.* 3, p. 261.)

And, when all is said and done, everything is summed up in the practice of the second commandment, for to be faithful to that is the most perfect and surest means of observing the first:

> The surest sign that we are keeping these two commandments is, I think, that we should really be loving our neighbour. . . . It is most important that we should proceed in this matter very carefully, for if we have attained great perfection here, we have done everything. Our nature being so evil, I do not believe we could ever attain perfect love for our neighbour unless it had its roots in the love of God.
>
> (*Ibid.*, pp. 251-2.)

In this St Teresa is simply echoing the teaching of St John and of Christ himself. The love of our neighbour, as he taught it to his apostles in the discourse after the Last Supper, is permanently *his* commandment and the sign by which those who are truly his disciples will be recognized. Might we not be tempted to show surprise at this, to think that Christ's primary purpose in coming was to teach us that the Father loves us and we must respond to his love? In point of fact the love of our neighbour is nothing else than the perfection, the fullness and radiance, of the Father's love. That is why Christ could find no better way of telling us that he was bringing us all the fullness of divine love, than by setting this commandment before us as his own.

To fulfil this command it is not adequate merely to resolve with a firm will to observe it faithfully. It is essential to enter into the spirit of it, to learn to set our relations with others on a new plane, in a new light—the light of Christ.

We are one in Christ, with not just any sort of unity, but so deeply inter-dependent one on another that in one sense we no longer have any exclusively personal interests. We are too deeply involved in a common destiny, which is that of the Mystical Body, to be able to separate our own destiny from it. Each of our acts has repercussions which it is impossible to measure; still less can we conceive our debt to this unity in which we have our place—the life of the whole Church which supports our effort.

We are all engaged in the same work, in the same sort of conditions—all of us are at grips with our human frailty, which has need of indulgence, comprehension and support. We have to bring help to one another, to support one another in these difficulties which are common to us all. We are enveloped by the mystery of divine mercy and the more we enter into the spirit of that mercy, the more freely will our life grow in the only atmosphere in which it can expand.

Humility and Patience

Charity is merciful, is patient. That is why it is the source of peace. Peace cannot be arrived at by making an effort to get rid of the causes of irritation. We may be tempted, when we think what disturbance is sometimes caused by the most trivial occasion of impatience, to wonder whether we can possibly avoid it except by fleeing from the distressing circumstances which stir up such storms. That, however, is not how to arrive at true peace of soul, which, writes the author of the *Imitation*, 'consists in suffering humbly, rather than in not feeling what vexes us'. It is by struggling to the best of our ability, with simplicity and perseverance, without being discouraged if the results seem at first not to correspond in any way to so much effort, that we shall see these difficulties grow less. The soul will gradually become peaceful and will learn to find its joy in sweetness and patience and to taste therein the secret savour of humility, which is hidden in them.

For there is a very close link between humility and patience. At the roots of each outburst of irritation or anger, if we look closely, it is easy to discover a reaction of wounded self-love. The thing that hurts is not that we must put up with some little inconvenience, often very slight, but that this is imposed upon us by others. That is why we feel so much more vexed when men thwart us, than if events do so. People make use of us without our consent. Someone else claims to impose his will upon us, and we will not accept it precisely because it is his will and he is substituting it for ours. This wounds our independence and we feel no humiliation more deeply. Yet none is more profitable to us. 'Learn to humble thyself,' writes the author of the *Imitation*, 'and to offer thyself to every kind of dependence.' And St Jeanne de Chantal, enquiring what virtues we can practise with the greatest profit, answers: 'Submissiveness and obedience, for the greatest acts of humility are found in submission. It is the touchstone for recognizing whether the sanctity and humility found in a soul are genuine.' This is a much more effective way to make progress in true self-denial than mortifications, which are more painful in themselves, but which do not entail this effort to submit to others. This submission, in fact, wounds our self-love in its centre, which is where it must be struck if we are to dislodge the hard and rugged rock of self-attachment.

For this is precisely what is at stake. This pride, which refuses to yield, is the root cause of our feelings of impatience and it is pride again which maintains and envenoms them. If the agitation caused by an incident persists, and we are kept in a state of irritation, it is because, in one way or another, our self-love is suffering from a wound that has not healed properly. We have had to yield, to accept the fact that circumstances seem to have proved us wrong, or that others have been able to impose upon us their own, possibly arbitrary way of looking at things. We have lost. The day we succeed in accepting, with true interior liberty, this sort of frustration—and this is not weakness but rather self-mastery which lets us dominate a great deal of triviality—patience will become easy for us. We may still let slip sudden movements of irritation, but we shall be free from the real disturbances, which extend and destroy the peace of the soul.

This will be the means, too, of preserving harmony with all and of quickly cutting short any dissension. Things would go so easily if only we would act with a little more simplicity and humility, not wait to be reconciled with someone who has offended us no matter how slightly, until he admits how far he is in the wrong—or until we have succeeded in proving to him that we are in the right—as if there were no better ways to pacify him than to prove the flimsiness of his complaints. . . .

On the contrary, surely the best way to calm someone who is irritated with us, is to acknowledge whatever justification there may be in his reproaches. To explain, to try to sort things out, can only be effective in so far as we admit the greatest share of wrong to be ours, leaving it to the other party to acknowledge his own wrongs in his turn, after we have in this way helped him to do so.

Humility is hence the first condition of patience—and consequently of charity. It is, however, a difficult virtue; to practise it, we must sincerely love it. It is before God in prayer that we come to see how beneficial it is, how good it is to dwell therein, finding in it everything desirable and true peace of soul. For humility prepares the ways of grace, smoothing out the obstacles in its path, the hard, resisting points of pride and selfishness, of self-assertion, which refuse to mould themselves in supple docility to the action of grace.

Humility may reveal the best of itself in prayer, but no one will succeed in truly loving this virtue, if he does not practise fidelity to it on those occasions when charity, and above all patient charity, lets him do so, in a discreet manner, hidden from the eyes of men, not attracting praise, but in self-effacement, avoiding all self-assertion. Such is the humility which we must love—humility simple and hidden, purest and most genuine. It is this that strips us most deeply of self, and only this expands freely in the joy of the love of God.

A truly humble soul has no thought except for God. Faced with a temptation to impatience it will say, with complete sincerity, that it is vain to dwell on what hurts only itself. It is not worth further thought, not worth turning one's gaze aside from God for that.

For that is what a loving soul needs—self-effacement, total humility, all attention to itself to disappear in the desire to be entirely given up to him it loves.

Mercy

Yet again, humility is patient and sweet. It knows how much we ourselves have been forgiven and thus is prompt to indulgence.

Far from wanting to settle accounts in strict justice with its neighbours, it thinks rather of the account it must itself settle with God. He has forgiven us so much that we should love to acknowledge the abundance of his mercies by forgiving in our turn. St Teresa of Avila writes that the soul truly favoured by God, though it has not equal strength

> for the practice of the other virtues will at least have it for that of forgiving injuries. I cannot believe, that a soul so intimately united to infinite mercy, in which it recognizes its nothingness and sees how much God has forgiven it, will not immediately pardon, with the greatest ease, and will not experience the most charitable feelings for him who has injured it. It sees in the graces and favours with which God has overwhelmed it such pledges of love that it rejoices to find an

opportunity to show him some mark of the love which it has for him (*Way of Perfection,* ch. 38).

To be indulgent towards others' weaknesses is to act as God himself acts, having one mind with him. There is no better means of learning how prompt he is to pardon and have compassion, or with what humble confidence we should live in his presence.

If we see a man, who has lapsed, regretting his fault, and find in him the good will and desire to do better, we can no longer see anything but this good will, even if it admits that it is very weak and uncertain of triumphing; our one desire is to help it. That is the way God looks upon us, in our numerous daily failings, if each time, we humbly go on trying. Following his example, that is how we should look upon those who have injured us in some way. Their fault, even if we suspect a certain hidden malice mixed with it, springs at bottom from weakness. To let it irritate us would be to lose our unity of sentiment with God. The man whom we regard with anger he looks upon with mercy, with that divine condescension which never abandons the sinner but plies him with the appeals of grace, seeking by a thousand means to bring him to repentance.

'God is rich in mercy and slow to anger.' God is infinitely perfect, but his perfection, far from being a matter of fear for us, is on the contrary the surest foundation of our hope. In fact, the more perfect God's justice, the more merciful it is. It is surely a more difficult and delicate thing to be compassionate than to practise a rigorous severity, to understand other people's weaknesses and be indulgent to them, than to condemn them according to the laws of strict justice. Moreover, Christ, though he inveighs against the hardness and pride of the Pharisees, has only gentleness and pardon—never a harsh word—for faults of weakness, even the most serious ones, in the case of poor souls struggling against their human frailty?

People sometimes speak of God's severity, but is not even this a form of his mercy? He is said to be more severe towards those he loves; but if he seems to punish them more harshly, is it not just that he insists, with greater persistence, on making them hear the calls of his grace in order to lead them back to him. For his love has no second thought. He asks more of those to whom he has given most, but this does not mean that he is more ready to be angered by their infidelities and to abandon them to themselves; but, rather, he pursues them further with the requirements of his unrepentant love. As St Teresa says:

> Let the soul trust in the goodness of God, which is greater than all the evil. When, with full knowledge of ourselves, we desire to return to friendship with Him, He remembers neither our ingratitude nor our misuse of the favours that He has granted us. He might well chastise us for these sins, but in fact He makes use of them only to forgive us the more readily, just as He would forgive those who have been members of His household and who, as they say, have eaten of His bread.
>
> (*Life*, ch. 19.)

Such are the infinite riches of the divine mercy, of

which at least some reflection should shine in our attitude towards our neighbour. It is not enough to be good—the goodness which *gives* is that of the world at large; it is so natural to like to do good, particularly to those who suffer or are weak. Moreover, in the practice of this protective kindness, we are not proof against the secret pleasure of exercising superiority. More unusual, however, is the goodness which *forgives*; and yet that is true goodness, humble, stripped of any return to self, true, conquering goodness which always ends by having the last word, before which every obstacle eventually gives way.

To know how to forgive is to enter into God's plan and to further it, for our pardon draws down his; more than that, his pardon is transmitted through our own, which only sheds forth for others the mercy with which God surrounds us and asks us to share with our brethren. Surely a much more satisfactory way for us to find compensation for the wrongs which others have done us than by humiliating the one who has injured us, lies in the joy of forgiving him and thereby drawing down upon him God's own pardon, and helping him to respond to that divine mercy, truly to believe in it by bringing it home to him in a form that is sensible, accessible, made real to him by our own pardon.

Perhaps God had foreseen that his grace would come to this soul by this particular channel—for always, simply because he can thereby do more for us, he is pleased to realize his designs through us, making them depend on our co-operation—in this his love shows a very delicate attention towards us, and it is well worth forgetting our susceptibilities and our claims in order to respond to it, losing them in our single-minded anxiety to help our brethren, to be more closely united with them in the carrying out of the common work.

Gift and Pardon

To help our neighbour we must first of all show indulgence and kindness towards him. But should we take care not to go too far? Surely it is important that he who has acted badly should realize the fact. Is it really doing him a service to seem to ignore his wrong doing? We consider it might be useful to bring them discreetly home to him.

But, in the first place, we need only be slightly attentive to others to understand that they are much more aware of their faults and feel the burden of them much more heavily than we think. Even those who seem strongest feel their human weakness, their limitations, and suffer from them all the more keenly, the more they take pride in self-assurance and the assertion of their superiority. Other people's faults do not get off as lightly as we imagine and, if we realized this better, it should incline us to indulgence. Compassion is the best antidote to impatience; it would be our first reaction if only we could see how often we touch people on the quick and crush them under a burden already heavy to bear, when we lay stress on their shortcomings.

Moreover, there is always someone ready to perform this office, to help our neighbour see his wrong-doings; it is not so easy to find someone to offer kindly and understanding help. Thus it is better to choose this second task, and to rely upon others, if needs be, to take on the first which in any case is full of pitfalls!

God himself should be our example in this. How prudently his grace acts when it enlightens us as to our faults, gradually enlightening us in the measure in which we can bear it, knowing how to be patient, how to wait for the opportune moment! It is surely presumption to want to intervene of our own initiative in so infinitely delicate a work. To do so to good purpose, it would be necessary to act with so much charity, prudence and, above all, purity of intention. We would need to be quite sure that we were not letting passion carry us away to some excess or clumsiness. Thus it is wise to refrain as soon as there is any cause to suspect ourselves of a secret wish, concealed in the desire of making another realize his wrong-doings, to force him to confess the wrong he has done towards us: an unavowed need to see the one who has failed us, if he is not punished for it in any other way, at least suffer the embarrassment of having to own himself guilty.

It is not surprising, when we are more or less consciously driven by motives like these, that we arrive at such wretched results. Far from helping others to discern their faults, such methods only make it even harder for them to be sincere towards themselves; unless they are truly very virtuous, it will only make them less inclined to recognize where the fault lies. We all find it less easy to admit the grounds for a reproach that is made to us, even justly and in all charity, by someone else than to admit our errors spontaneously? All the more so if the intention of the one who thinks himself justified in reproving us appears less pure than it might be.

A little indulgent kindness would be a much more effective means of winning the goodwill of all, even of those who seem the least persuaded to yield. For charity is the virtue most immediately rewarded here on earth—our neighbour, too, knows how to repay a hundredfold. If we would only try to practise sweetness with some measure of perseverance, the result would astonish us. A little more kindness towards those whose attitude is less lovable, might suffice to make them feel the contrast between their way of acting and the kindness which is shown to them? Then they should realize what is lacking in their way of life, should feel genuine shame for it and the desire to be forgiven. They would become sweeter of their own accord. The wolves would become lambs. Resistance which seemed impossible to overcome would yield without effort.

That is the way in which we could help others to be good . . . and the way in which also, perhaps, we should discover with joy that they are better than we thought.

Here more than anywhere else there is a striking contrast between the inevitable frustration of human means and the supernatural effectiveness of patience, of gentleness which knows how to wait and hope without becoming weary, because it believes in goodness, wills to believe in it in the face of and against everything. Trusting to God's hands, in an act of surrender, the pain we feel at the misunderstandings and frustrations met with in our relations with others, or at any humiliation which we have suffered, we feel re-assured. We know that in all this it is still God who is putting us to the test and if we rest patiently and submissively in his hands, he will lead us to that true peace which is not attained by imposing our points of view, by getting the upper hand of an opponent, but by the triumph of God's grace alone and of his charity. The soul progresses all the more surely towards this peace because, in this surrender which frees it from any personal preoccupation, from any thought of gain, it is easier to act with purity of intention, with complete disinterest.

For charity cannot be beneficial if it is not self-forgetful and truly marked by the gift of self.

We must altogether renounce the idea of dealing with our neighbours on the basis of a strict balance of justice. There can be no question of admitting an occasional exception to the rigour of this law, while maintaining our right to demand what is due to us, the law of justice all the while remaining the fundamental rule of our mutual relations. That would be inadequate. Our relations with our neighbour must be ruled by a different law—the law of utter self-giving which is that of love. For love knows nothing of mine and thine. It is free from such fetters. It is prompt to give, to give ever more, or even to let others take, which is as it were a more perfect and deeper way of giving.

Surely it is important that all men should have their share of joy? Our own joy . . . the more we feel we have found it in God, the more we shall desire to do what lies in our power to give each one his own joy. To give it, or let it be taken, even if it is at our own expense and not perhaps without some embarrassment. We must learn to accept these small infringements with a good will, learn to forget ourselves in order to help our neighbour find what he needs to expand, to bear the burden of life, often heavier than we imagine, more joyfully.

To give joy is the best means of doing good; like any other life, the spiritual life can expand only in peace and happiness. To help others find this happiness is to help them draw close to God, to believe in his love which in this way becomes more real for them.

And for ourselves, it is good to feel that we have given joy, especially to people who have so little of it! And they are the ones that it is easiest to give it to—a mere trifle moves them to the depths of their hearts.

Since the love of our neighbour is so close to the love of God, it cannot fail to be, as he is, the source of most sweet joy; it spreads a profusion of joy wherever it passes.

Kindliness of judgement

How are we to be truly charitable towards our neighbour without first learning to judge him with kindness, to look sympathetically upon his efforts to do better, knowing, if need be, how to shut our eyes with loving kindness to his failings?

Instead of always clashing with people's disagreeable sides, why not try rather to understand what each of us has that is good, and approach from that angle. How ashamed we sometimes feel at having by-passed genuine virtues without seeing them, because we were brought up short by small points and the disturbance or irritation they occasioned in us. In this way a slight fault is sometimes enough to blind us to great qualities. As to faults, we all have them. That is a situation we have to accept as it is, the condition in which we have to sanctify ourselves together, in patience and mutual support. There is no question of denying their existence, but these imperfections must not prevent us from recognizing, or even lead us to depise, the work which grace is accomplishing in every soul. 'Do not judge someone from the point of view of the virtues you would like to see in him,' writes St John of the Cross, 'think that he can be very pleasing to God for reasons of which you have no idea.'

Moreover, the best means of understanding others' weaknesses and of showing compassion for them is surely to acquire a more exact awareness of our own shortcomings? If we were sincerely humble, conscious of our own poverty, knew how to judge ourselves, we would no longer find it possible to pass severe judgement on our neighbour, for we should find in ourselves something which would prevent this.

Our faults, says St Teresa of Avila, should be like a veil drawn over our eyes, to prevent us from seeing those of others.

To judge another with kindness is not to shut our eyes so that we may not see, but perhaps, on the contrary, to purify our vision in order to make it more far-sighted. It is not a matter of persuading ourselves at all costs that our neighbour is not guilty of the faults which he obviously has, but rather to understand that after having taken away everything which excuses them, not a great deal remains, as a rule—so little that the best thing would be to act as if they did not exist, to pay no attention to them. So and so, for instance, whose character seems difficult to put up with.... Isn't it that he has simply missed his share of joy which would have made him more kindly, more responsive? And someone else, so touchy, whose self-love is so quickly wounded, has he not had to bear frustrations which have made him feel his limitations and inferiority too painfully, so that the slightest knock re-opens the wound?

To restore just measure to our evaluations we must, moreover, take into account not only what excuses our neighbour, but also all that inclines *us* to severity. It is so easy to let ourselves be carried away when we are passing judgement by a feeling of annoyance or irritation or, again, to exaggerate the importance of a fault which, though it may not be serious in itself, has the misfortune to jar with the most marked tendencies of our own temperament . . . tendencies to which we cling the more strongly because our personality finds it easier to assert and impose itself through them. For that very reason they please other people less and they would be grateful to us if we displayed them with a little more discretion.

So it is prudent not to show ourselves too eager to pronounce judgement, to blame the conduct of our neighbour; otherwise we shall always find something to criticize, even among the best, were it only ways of acting or thinking which come into conflict with what we have derived from our upbringing the milieu in which we have lived.

It is because they spied on him in that way, in the light of their own prejudices, that the Pharisees continually found—and perhaps, at times, in good faith—things to reprove in Christ himself. They merely acted towards him as we all too often do in regard to our neighbour, considering him with regard that has little kindness in it, with that pharisaical glance which makes us too pass by Christ, present in our brethren, without recognizing him.

Yet how good it is to learn to recognize Christ in our brethren, to take pleasure in rejoicing at the good that is in them! That is how we respond to the kindly influence, the radiance of the good in others, and the soul expands in this feeling of very pure charity which sets it free, pacifies it, sweetens everything in it; to experience the delicate savour of this feeling would perhaps be enough to make us renounce for ever the bitterness of jealousy.

We must take more willing pleasure in seeing the good which is in others than the evil—it is surely by creating for ourselves through all that we learn to see or not to see around us, the atmosphere in which we live, that we make ourselves happy or miserable.

Peace and Grace

The spiritual life can expand only in an atmosphere of charity. That is why it is important to dwell in peace with all, never to resign ourselves to a state of semi-hostility, or simply of coldness, with anyone whatsoever and to hold ourselves responsible for this state of affairs so long as we have not done all we could to bring it to an end. To do otherwise would be to move out of the stream of charity; we should no longer be carried along by it and our effort for good would be sterilized and lose its effectiveness.

Moreover, more often than we think, this could cause us not to recognize a good will fully prepared to show itself. A sharp gesture, a word of impatience which merely expresses a passing feeling, can be too readily interpreted as the sign of a more lasting animosity, and we attribute such feelings to one who already regrets his bad temper and wants only to make up for it? So little would be needed to encourage him in this and help him to do so more easily.

We must never dwell upon a painful incident. And sometimes just a pleasant word, the smallest sign of kindly understanding, is enough to restore peace to one who, perhaps, is worried, thinking us irritated, that he is no longer living in absolute charity with his neighbour.

For it is right that we should think of this too. We are not meant to practise charity only for ourselves, as an exercise of personal perfection, but to practise it sincerely for others, desiring to enable them to live in peace and joy and thus tend more easily towards God.

There is no better means of forgetting our small personal troubles, our susceptibilities, our clashes with others, than to transcend them in this way by occupying our minds on a higher level, and realizing more surely how greatly our charity to our neighbour will help him to find God.

Again if charity is beneficial to others, it is also beneficial to ourselves. It is the only source of peace.

The first condition, without which true peace is not to be found, is surely to purify our thoughts of everything that is opposed to charity. We must rid ourselves of the thousand trivial flaws that so easily insinuate themselves into the atmosphere of a soul prone to pay attention to such trifles, which should be by-passed, unseen. 'Do not harbour a suspicion unfavourable to your brother,' writes St John of the Cross, 'for suspicion takes away purity of heart.' It is so easy to give rein, without even noticing it, to seemingly unimportant movements of annoyance which are yet sufficient to maintain an interior acidity in which charity wilts and the soul cannot expand.

Often, it is largely just a matter of good sense and good humour—to be able to smile, with a genuine smile, at our neighbour's failings and oddities, instead of always being irritated at them; not to make an obstacle out of small things; to thrust aside our moments of impatience without examining them—or perhaps simply to humiliate ourselves, which implies a disavowal of them—this is how to remain in peace and destroy before they take shape many acts or words by which, one day or another, this irritation, kept alive by a thousand constantly fresh trifles, would secretly and perhaps unconsciously betray itself.

Charity is the means of guarding our peace, the means also of finding it again at times when we might think it lost. There are times when we feel surrounded by darkness or trouble; we cannot see how to recover our balance. Let the opportunity arise of showing some kindness to our neighbour and often nothing more is needed to restore our calm—the contact with grace has been found once more. For nowhere can it be better found than in an act of obedience to Christ's command—by doing as he bids us we correspond to the desire which Christ himself expressed, the desire dear among all others, to which a sincere love takes delight in responding with the utmost eagerness and most delicately attentive fidelity.

Love one another, for it is the Lord's command, and however little it may be accomplished, that suffices: si solum fiat, sufficit.

Love one another. To love solely for the joy of loving—it is good to love, because God is love and to love is to dwell in him.

To love our neighbour in this way is not to love him for the sake of another's love, but for what is deepest in himself; it is to recognize in him so intimate a link with God that God dwells in our love of our neighbour, and there is nowhere else that we may find him if we do not begin by seeking him there.

CHAPTER II

The austerity of the Cross

THERE is no love without sacrifice, no gift of self without self-forgetfulness. So love cannot be separated from the Cross—love's progress rests on the Cross.

The Cross is at the heart of the Christian mystery because it is a mystery of love, of redemptive love. Each day the Christian must bear his cross with Christ, that thereby may gradually be accomplished in him, through humble day-to-day opportunities for renunciation, a work of self-stripping which purifies him, frees him from the bonds of pride and of selfishness, and makes him responsive to the love of God, in order that this may gradually strengthen its sway in him and finally hold everything in perfect submission to it.

An austere path, certainly, a task hard and difficult, arduous enough swiftly to discourage anyone who might think he had to achieve it by relying on his own strength. But to try to realize it in that way would be to turn aside from the path traced out by Christ for his disciples—the yoke we were putting on our shoulders would no longer be his. In order to understand how much *his* yoke 'is sweet, and his burden light', we must put our hope in the Cross, in the grace which is in the Cross to purify every soul who yields to it with docility.

The task remains, with all it demands—as Christ carried his Cross, so we have to carry ours, which is our own but still his. To take anything away, would be to retract from our union with him. But it is he who will bear it in us, supporting us and giving redemptive value to our sacrifices just because that he unites them to his own. So they will no longer feel like a burden dumped on our shoulders, but like a gift of divine mercy—this is the way, opening before us, which leads us to God.

This way of the Cross is the only one by which, following in Christ's footsteps, we can penetrate with him the mystery to which he gives us access. John of the Cross says:

> Oh that it might be perfectly understood how the soul cannot attain to the thicket of the wisdom and riches of God save by entering into the thicket of many kinds of suffering . . . and how the soul that of a truth desires wisdom first desires truly to enter farther into the thicket of the Cross, which is the road of life, which few enter! For the desire to enter into the thicket of wisdom and riches and favours of God comes to all, but the desire to enter into the thicket of trials and pains, for the sake of the Son of God, comes to few. Thus many would fain see themselves at the end, without passing along the road and way thereto.
>
> (11 *Spiritual Canticle,* Stanza 35.)

The meaning of the sanctifying value of suffering is an essential aspect of the Christian spirit. To Peter, who wanted to turn him aside from the passion and Cross, Christ replied—'Get thee behind me, Satan, thou art a stumbling-block to me, for thou hast not the sense of the things of God, but that of the things of men.'

To have the sense of the things of men is to dread suffering and shun it as an evil! To have the sense of the things of God is to penetrate the mystery of the Cross, to recognize the redemptive value of suffering, and of the very least trials of daily life, born in union with Christ.

To want too easy a life where everything happens in accordance with our desires would be to thrust aside opportunities of grace, would be to thrust aside grace itself, by refusing to enter into the ways of God and accept the means chosen by him for the realization of the work he has entrusted to us, which is our only true interest.

What we must consider is the task to be accomplished, without any other concern than to carry it out well, faithfully and with courage. Either we accept its austerity, without fearing the suffering, or, if we seek to enjoy tranquillity nothing is left us but to resign ourselves to the emptiness of a mediocre existence. This truth is clearly impressed upon us when, in the course of some trial we have anticipated with dread, we see that what it brings is a great deal more to be prized than what it deprives us of, and that it is far better that everything should not have turned out in accordance with our desires?

Suffering and Truth

Of necessity, we must find the Cross in our path. Frustrations or disappointments, far from obstructing us, yield more fruit than joys and successes do. At times of happiness, indeed, we enjoy a tranquillity, the artificiality of which we do not realize. We are satisfied; we feel the need of nothing else. Doubtless the happiness we taste at such times is fragile, but it is sweet too and it is very natural to rest in it. Once this joy is taken away from us, the false security vanishes, the frail equilibrium is already broken and we start trying to find once more the peace we have lost . . . we search, we become conscious of a need, which can only be satisfied in God, and that is why already we are on the road that leads to him. Often enough we turn to God when all else has come to fail us. And if this is true of the great trials which determine great conversions, it is true also of the small daily trials which occasion those small conversions by which our progress towards God becomes firmer and more secure?

Suffering brings us to the heart of things. In the well-being of times of happiness we live on the surface of life, we delude ourselves as to the value of our feelings. Our inner attitude can scarcely be called generous, but all the same it is adequate for easy circumstances; we do not feel the need of making a greater effort; we are at peace as we are. When we are faced by a trial, then God's demands become clear, we understand what he asks of a soul in order to draw it to him, and that, if we mean to attain the goal towards which we thought we were travelling along that easy road, we must achieve a detachment from self, an interior self-stripping from which we feel far removed. Then we realize that we are entangled in the bonds of these human joys, which made us so comfortable and whose sudden privation throws us into consternation. Then we see what our heart is really like. It seems as if the veil has been torn aside and the whole spiritual life shows forth in a new light, as a reality more austere, but how much more beautiful and more profound; the way of new progress opens before us. By withdrawing from us the joys, which more or less consciously we made the objective of our life, suffering forces us to turn back towards the only happiness to which it leaves access—towards God. It shows in him the only end we should pursue, it teaches us to consider the rest solely as means and to prefer, among these means, the most effective, even if they ask more of us.

This does not mean that we must necessarily come to prefer always what is most painful, for that would be out of proportion to our strength, excessive and presumptuous; but neither must we wish everything to succeed with us; we must simply desire God to be able to realize his plan. This humble and peaceful submission, this attitude of surrender, made up of self-effacement before God and faith in his goodness, is what suffering leads us to.

Suffering and Humility

The work of our sanctification remains difficult and austere. It cannot be achieved except by sacrifice, and if it is to have a satisfactory end, it is essential for us to resolve to arrive at the goal at all costs and, once begun, not to abandon the task on any pretext. Sometimes everything will seem to fail us and we shall begin to wonder whether God himself has not forsaken us, whether we are attempting the impossible in pursuing a perfection which seems so remote, so far beyond our strength. The idea may then enter our mind to leave a road that really is far too arduous, and perhaps it is only because there is no other road, and that apart from God there is no issue, that we shall return to him, saying as St Peter did—'Lord, to whom shall we go? Thou hast the words of eternal life.' And we shall find once more the courage which seemed on the point of deserting us in the thought that, though the task is difficult, God has given us a means of accomplishing it, all the same, in peace and joy: humility, which is born of suffering.

Those with whom everything succeeds still keep their rock of self-confidence intact and are in danger, at the first frustration, of finding themselves a prey to troubles which are the fruit of pride and lead to discouragement. On the contrary, the soul whom suffering humbly endured has gradually softened enjoys great peace, it perseveres with simplicity in the task it has undertaken, without being surprised at its weakness; it pursues its efforts, telling itself that, amidst all the imperfections in which they seem buried God will find the poor tokens of love it offers him. It knows that grace is merciful enough to sustain our good will with a patience that nothing wearies.

Not only is it at peace, but through a continual act of faith in God's goodness it is able to find, on the austere path it has to climb, enough joy to expand.

It can be said that it no longer endures real suffering—not that it no longer feels pain, but there is no longer anything bitter in its suffering, nothing which disconcerts it. It submits in peace and surrender. It comes to look upon suffering as a friend, the messenger of God from whose hands it receives it.

Doubtless a trial that is sharper than usual can still bring pain, or arouse in it a storm which, without disturbing its most intimate depths, scarcely allow it any longer to discern the peace which lies concealed therein. But God sees the secret peace which is the fruit of his grace and the proof that his love is alive in this soul.

'Blessed are the humble,' writes the author of the *Imitation,* 'for they shall enjoy great peace.'

Suffering and Love

Suffering is a means of sanctification, not just any means which we may use or not use, which we may choose or spurn for another, but a necessary, essential means. There is no sanctification apart from sharing in the mystery of the Cross, apart from sacrifice, which alone can deepen our love of God by giving us the opportunity to exert our love in a more entire, more sincere self giving. Thus any tendency to minimise the rôle of the Cross and the redemptive character of grace must be viewed with the utmost reserve.

It none the less remains true that it is primarily the Holy Spirit who acts in us and suffering is only a means, an instrument of grace, an instrument which grace uses, moreover, with complete freedom. The purifying action which it accomplishes in a soul does not always correspond to the importance of the sacrifices which have been the occasion of it.

The share of suffering which each of us will have to undergo will depend, therefore, on the work God wants to effect in him, with the peculiar characteristics, and special conditions, and everything else which constitutes personal vocation. God has his plan for each soul, and in this plan he gives suffering its place, according to his intentions.

We must be docilely amenable to these intentions of God: our attitude in regard to suffering—or to any trouble—should thus be primarily an attitude of acceptance, welcoming with simplicity what God himself sends us.

This does not exclude voluntary mortification; the distinction, moreover, is not always clear-cut. Did some sacrifice freely consented to, turn up by itself, or was it providentially placed there as an opportunity for us to strive to free ourselves from an ill-mortified attachment? Accordingly, surely the fact that we do not evade it is simple docility to God's guidance of us. And on the other hand, to welcome eagerly and with a right good will, as a means of progressing in his love, any suffering that God himself imposes, is surely to offer it as a voluntary and spontaneous sacrifice.

But when we look at it like this mortification no longer seems a methodical exercise for us to use at our own discretion. It is rather an attitude of docility to God's guidance, of a vigilance eager to respond to the least of his wishes. Hence we are called upon to practise it in a way that is freer, simpler, but not less generous—very much to the contrary. The more aware we grow that a divine plan is being accomplished in our life, and that each of our acts has its place in it, the more careful we shall be to fit in with God's design and not to upset its execution by our failure to do so. We shall seek to make ourselves docile and supple. If heavier trials are sent to us, it is to grace that we shall look for the strength to bear them, and if we are spared them, we shall feel even more bound to welcome eagerly the petty trials of each day, to manifest by so doing our esteem for sacrifice which makes us share in the Cross, our desire to remain always close to this sole source of life, this mystery in which Christ is present and unites himself to us.

This is the way to dwell in this spirit of renunciation which is an essential part of the Christian spirit. It is the way, too, to keep ourselves prepared to consent generously to the more considerable sacrifices which God may perhaps need to demand, at one time or another, in order that we may make new progress in his love.

Suffering and Redemption

We lend ourselves in this way to the accomplishment of the mystery of the redemption, in ourselves and in others. Christ is the only one in whom suffering has been redemptive solely for others. In us, the sacrifices which we have to offer in union with, and for the Church, always remain for ourselves primarily the instrument of a never completed process of purification.

To lend ourselves with docility to the action of grace accomplishing in each of us its redemptive work, is to work for the redemption of the world, to strive to make more present in the world, more active, the divine leaven which has power to transform it—grace, the fruit of Christ's unique sacrifice, which he alone has merited for all of us, which is diffused in his mystical Body to the extent that each of its members surrenders himself to it, leaving it freedom to act in him.

Our every act of renunciation co-operates the more effectively in this work of universal redemption to the extent that it is effective in achieving our own redemption, in effecting that interior purification by which grace is enabled to take more and more complete possession of our soul. For a soul which is so possessed is like a presence, a point of insertion of grace in the world. The soul no longer acts; it gives grace the opportunity to act, invites it, draws it down upon souls by its every word and action, its every desire. That is why its efforts bear fruit *in patientia*—in patience and in faith, faith which refuses to be troubled by apparent frustrations, for it knows that it is essential to let God do what he wills.

The struggle in which we find ourselves engaged is a difficult one—it is the work of the world's redemption. God, if he had willed it, could have accomplished this by the simple affirmation and triumph of the all-powerfulness of his grace. This way of power was the very temptation by which Christ, in the wilderness, was tried in vain, which perhaps explains why it cannot be the way of God. To carry out the mystery of his love, he has chosen more humble means—he has preferred to take man as he was, at grips with the sin that is in him, with his infirmities, his ignorance, and accomplish in him a work which, instead of overcoming these obstacles at a single stroke, surmounts them gradually, taking into account the conditions in which we find ourselves and the more or less generous co-operation that we give him. This poor human co-operation, with its inadequacies and its failures, is a very imperfect second to grace, and does not allow grace its full power of expansion. It lends itself rather to the slow, hidden, modest work of patience. It is the humility of the Cross, which Christ lives over again in each one of his members. It is the law that binds us all, in accordance with which our progress towards God is accomplished. It applies to those who, plunged in and completely caught up by earthly preoccupations, unable to get free in order to raise themselves higher, show no signs of aspiring towards anything else and seem to be in almost invincible ignorance of a world which is as it were closed to them. But it applies also to the saints themselves—God leads them only gradually to a truer and deeper understanding of these divine realities, an understanding to which they cannot attain except by the slow work of purifying grace which strips them, too, of their human coarseness.

It is essential to bear in mind this difficulty inherent in the struggle in which we are engaged, if we are to understand what a generous effort it demands of us, and not let ourselves be discouraged by the sacrifices and share of suffering which it necessarily involves.

This is all the more true since our co-operation in this work of the redemption, like all the aspects of this mystery, is a much more profound matter than we suspect.

The unfathomable riches of divine mercy are revealed in the redemption, and they are made manifest under a thousand different forms, whose secret magnificence we could not possibly exhaust.

Nowhere do they appear more strikingly than in the most pure soul of the Virgin Mary, raised to the heights of sanctity befitting her divine Motherhood, by a grace which remains a grace of redemption, a grace which is wholly merciful.

But if our gaze cannot rise high enough to contemplate these splendours, neither can it be sufficiently penetrating to plumb the depths where, again, the uttermost limits of divine mercy are expressed with the same inexhaustible profusion. For God displays his overflowing abundance both in the munificence of his gifts and by deigning to stoop to the gulf of our wretchedness.

Let us consider those who have to bear more heavily than others the weight of the sin from which Christ came to deliver us. Both within them, and in their environment, how many things are in league to make their path towards God difficult! In lives outwardly so humanly wretched, so little directed towards heaven, how can God be present? And yet, if the grace of redemption is truly offered to all, it must be able to find a means to come even to souls like these and succour their distress, in such a way that they find it accessible and morally possible to welcome and profit by it. We must, then, believe that in these lives there will occur at least enough good will, enough good desires for a faint gesture of appeal towards God, enough to express a little of the need and aspiration which opens a soul to the redeeming grace of Christ; this may be negligible in itself, perhaps, but it comes from a soul too heavily loaded with the weight of sin to be morally able to do much by its own efforts to set itself free. This glimmer of good will is sufficient to afford a foothold for that grace whose function is to cure the sinful world, to make up for its insufficiencies. We are surely bound to consider this redeeming grace in the light of the world it must ransom, and think it powerful enough to overcome the domination of sin wherever it is found. Is there any other way for the redemption to be effective for the greater part of humanity than by not only bringing support, help and pardon, but also by making up, in its mercy, for all that is wanting to feeble souls, who can scarcely make the faintest gesture of good will towards a God of whom perhaps they know nothing, whose lives are not necessarily bad, but give so little place to the love of God and seem to be so empty of him?

Taken individually, these lives seem very little inspired by the love of God, but this little, not, perhaps, sufficient to give them a value in themselves, is surely sufficient to give them some claim to be assumed into a whole, into that whole, animated by divine charity, which is the mystical body of Christ, and with which in this way they find themselves integrated, which supports them and raises them above themselves?

Moreover, a mystery of divine substitution is surely an essential aspect of the redemption? Christ acts on our behalf, for he has made himself one with us, but he also wills that we should act for one another. For everything in him is common to us. And the overflowing abundance of life that we receive from him and in which which is the mystical body of Christ, and with which in this way they find themselves integrated, which supports them and raises them above themselves?

Since this is the case, we could in no way be held responsible only for ourselves. This poverty, these infirmities which we see in others are our own—the grace which is in us, is in us in order to provide a remedy for them, and had we been more faithful to it, they would perhaps not be what they are, or not to the same extent.

The more generously this redemptive grace is granted

us, the more responsible we are for it, the more it is incumbent upon us to make it, as far as it depends on us, operative in this world which it wills to save.

CHAPTER III

The Cross, mystery of obedience

IN CRUCE VITA. The Cross of Christ, of the risen Christ, is the sole source of life; from this flows every grace by whatever channel it comes down to us.

That is why it is not possible for the mystery of the death and resurrection of Christ to be just the mystery, great and solemn above all mysteries, towards which our gaze turns in the heavy hours when a more serious trial afflicts us and when, since suffering now makes its presence felt too painfully, we feel that we can no longer bear it alone.

The Cross would not occupy the place it has in our life if it were only met with in those privileged moments when a more difficult sacrifice is demanded of us, the sort of sacrifice which we call a 'cross' precisely because it seems to make us suffer severely enough to deserve to be considered a means of entering with our Saviour into the mystery of his Passion and death, of reliving it in union with him or, rather, of offering ourselves to him in order that he may relive it in us who are his members.

Our whole existence should be a participation in the death and resurrection of Christ. This is an everyday mystery, the daily bread of the Christian life. It is the bread distributed each morning at the Eucharistic table where, in the very act of the redeeming sacrifice, renewed upon the altar, the Lord unites himself to his members, bringing them to a more intimate participation in the unique mystery in which their union with him is effected. It is the bread with which our soul is nourished, whence it draws a new life, which should be expressed in all its acts and give them a deeper meaning. What constitutes the real value of the existence of the Christian is that it is taken up and enveloped in the mystery of death and resurrection which Christ lives over again in each one of us, the mystery of our salvation, the sole mystery of salvation. *O crux, ave, spes unica!*

But how can this be? What proportion is there between these modest, trifling sacrifices which make up our daily fidelity to our Christian vocation, and the painful death, the absolute desolation of Christ crucified—'Father, why hast thou forsaken me?' Do we really relive this divine Passion when we accept willingly some particular inconvenience, some annoyance, some trouble which could not be called suffering, by going so far, if we must, as to bear without too much ill humour some humiliation, or the necessity of bending our own will and judgement to those of another? How can we make of the Cross an everyday reality without giving to very humble occasions of renunciation a quite disproportionate importance?

The point is that the Cross is not only the bloody immolation on which our imagination first siezes, the mystery of suffering in which we love to recognize the supreme witness of Christ's love for his Father, and at the same time the most manifest sign of his love for us, a sign which speaks to us the language we can most easily understand.

The mystery incarnate in the Passion of our Lord is a mystery of humiliation, a mystery of obedience—'Christ became for us obedient unto death, even to the death of the Cross' (Phil. 2, 8). This saying of St Paul links up with that which Scripture puts on the lips of Christ coming into this world—'Here I am, O God, I come to do thy will' (Heb. 10, 7). These two phrases hold between them all the earthly life of the Word Incarnate. And we continually find in the Gospels the reminder of that first intention, that perfect submission to the Father's will. . . .

Christ is the great model of obedience—'my meet is to do the will of him who sent me and to accomplish his work' (John. 4, 34). On several occasions this allusion to 'him who sent him' whose will he must follow in all things is repeated. It was for this purpose that he came among us—his earthly life has no other *raison d'être* than to accomplish a mission received from the Father, a mission which he must fulfil just as it has been committed to him—'I came down from heaven not to do my will, but the will of him who sent me. . . . I do not seek my will but the will of him who sent me' (John 6, 38; 5, 30). All these sayings reflect the calm serenity of one who knows that a task has been entrusted to him and that only one thing counts—to fulfil it faithfully. And when the last hour comes, all will be summed up in those perfectly simple words, through which can be read, behind the declaration that the work is now finished and the command accomplished, the expression, the deeper for being so restrained, of perfect love and of an unreserved gift of self: 'I have glorified thee upon earth in accomplishing the work that thou gavest me to do' (John 17, 4).

'If you keep my commandments you will remain in my love as I myself have kept the commandments of my Father and remain in his love' (John 15, 10). Christ teaches us by his example that obedience is the supreme means of remaining in the love of the Father and making it incarnate in our lives. He practised this obedience with the supreme liberty which is his and which we, as we shall see, can in some manner imitate.

No one can force him—so long as the moment fixed by the Father has not come, he hides himself—'They then sought to arrest him, but no one laid a hand on him because his hour had not yet come' (John 7, 30). When finally that hour came in which the final act of submission, the supreme proof of his love, was demanded of him, he gave it freely, without constraint, simply because he loved the Father and willed to accomplish his commands in everything. 'The Prince of this world cometh. Against me, indeed, he can do nothing, but it is essential that the world know that I love the Father and that I do what the Father has commanded me.' (John 14, 31.) And it is to this act of obedience that the love of the Father responds—'If the Father loves me, it is that I give up my life to take it again one day. No one takes it away from me, I give it up of myself. I have power to lay it down and power to take it up again—such is the command I have received from my Father' (John 10, 17 and 18).

The secret of Christ's perfect liberty is his union with the Father— Verily, verily, I say unto you, the Son can do nothing of himself, but only what he sees the Father do; what the Father does, the Son also does in like manner' (John 5, 19). In the secret of the intimate life of the Trinity, the Father and Son are one, and if the Son can do nothing of himself, nothing of which the Father is not the principle, it is also true that all that the Father does, the Son does in like manner, in perfect equality. This saying of Christ, however, applies primarily to his human acts, whose divine origin had to be demonstrated in the face of the attacks of the Jews. It is also true that Christ accomplishes these human acts with his human will, in a mysterious union with the Father, who makes of his obedience, of the submission of his will to the Father's will, a mystery which we can only adore. But, our own submission must be in the image and likeness of this mystery, for, animated by the grace of a divine life we too are, in Christ, children of the Father, one with him—'As thou, Father, thou art in me and I in thee, so may they also be one in us' (John 17, 21).

Here we find ourselves once more in the presence of this 'wonderful exchange' by which Christ, assuming our humanity, gives us a share in his divinity. For if our obedience, united to his, becomes in him a wholly new reality, his obedience becomes like unto ours, sharing in this human fragility of ours. Christ's submission to the Father's will is not impassiveness, not indifference to suffering. Like us, in the presence of this suffering, Christ trembles and shrinks, he experiences the 'weakness of the flesh', of our poor suffering flesh. His will, above all else, is that the will of his Father should be accomplished, but all the same he utters this prayer, which is not just a pretence intended to sustain and encourage our weakness in the hours of pain, but is truly the cry of his heart

—'Father, if thou wilt, let this chalice pass from me; nevertheless, not my will but thine be done.' (Luke 22, 42.) And there is a text of St John which gives even more strongly the impression of a struggle in his soul—'The hour is come when the Son of man should be glorified. . . . Now my soul is deeply troubled. What shall I say? Father, save me from this hour! But it is for this hour that I am come. Father, glorify thy name' (John 12, 23, 27, 28).

'It is precisely for this hour that I am come.' It was towards this act of supreme obedience that the Word Incarnate's whole life of submission tended. And he wants to associate us with this life, for this is what makes us his brethren: 'He who does the will of my Father who is in heaven, he is my brother and my sister and my mother' (Mt. 12, 50).

Following his example, let our meet be to accomplish the Father's will in all things; then, no longer living for ourselves, we shall find ourselves associated with the death of Christ and with his resurrection—'For the love of Christ urges us to the thought that, if one dies for all, all likewise are dead. And he died for all in order that the living may no longer live for themselves, but for him who died and rose again for them' (II Cor. 5, 14 and 15).

No longer to live for ourselves. The Christian cannot live for himself. He is engaged in a work that surpasses him—the work of Christ himself, the redemption of the world in which there is a job for him to do. He is a living stone shaped by the artisan's chisel, adapted by him for the place he has reserved for him in the building; a member whose growth cannot be kept separate from that of the body as a whole, the Christian is one with his brethren, he has to work with them at a common task. It can be said that his supernatural destiny is not an individual destiny—it is caught up in the destiny of the mystical body of Christ to the extent that, separated from that whole, it would lose all its meaning. As a member of Christ, he has to play, in the work that Christ has come to effect in this world, the part entrusted to him, wherein no other can stand in his stead.

Just as Christ's constant concern was to accomplish the will of his Father, the work for which he was sent, so the Christian's constant concern should be to accomplish, in union with Christ, the will of the Father for him personally. Just as he must find each of the mysteries of Christ in his life, so must he live the one which contains them all and which was consummated on Calvary—the mystery of his obedience.

To have no other concern than to accomplish the Father's will . . . or, better, to leave him to accomplish his will, to effect his plan—the design of his love—through the circumstances of our life.

For we are not meant to put our hands to a task entrusted to us so that, by our own means, by the strength of our arms we might bring it to completion. In that way we could only do what lay in our own strength, and that would remain purely natural, whereas it is to supernatural life that we are called.

This is not to say that we do not have to set to work, generously, with the means within our reach, to bring to completion as best we can, according to our strength and our lights, the work which is offered to us and to which we are called to apply ourselves. But it is important that we should know how to discern under these outward appearances the deeper truth that, beyond what we see or, rather, in this very reality of our daily labour, enlightened by a new light, faith causes us to discover that which gives its true meaning to our life.

It is true that we have a task to accomplish but through our fidelity to this task which he himself has chosen for us, through the various circumstances which come to bring us help and support or, on the contrary,—at least as it seems to us—to sow our path with obstacles which are perhaps disconcerting, it is God himself who leads us by a secret path, 'hidden as would be the traces of footsteps on the waters', according to the expression of St John of the Cross. This secret path is the only one, at rock bottom, on which it is important to make progress and its direction remains hidden from our eyes, under the entanglement of the paths along which we think we are advancing.

The important thing is not to choose one or another particular route, but to let ourselves be guided there by the hand which leads us and thus to learn a little better at each step how to surrender to this guiding hand, to follow it in docility, down every turning, in confidence.

For that is the testimony that God expects of us. Beneath all the other tasks at which we have to labour this is the primary work which it is important to perfect and from which the others draw their fruitfulness—we have to make our lives bear witness to trust in God. Such is our vocation, our vocation as men—faith, to live the love of God in faith. To make of our human existence this supreme testimony of love (in those whom we love, is not this what touches us most?), this supreme testimony of love which is an act of faith, of utter trust?

May God be able to read more clearly in each of our acts, each of our attitudes, this absolute, unconditional, unreserved trust of a soul which has faith in him and which he can lead where he wants, without its faith faltering.

So in the Christian's life will shine a reflection of that calm assurance which shows in Christ's actions and words in the Gospels and which finds its highest expression in the account of the Passion according to St John. It is St John also, who gives us the words of Christ which reveal the meaning and the profound source of this crowning peace: 'He who has sent me is with me. He has not left me alone, because I do always that which pleases him' (John 8, 29).

As Christ is in him, the Christian, if he endeavours to do the Father's will in all things, knows that the Father is with him and that he is secure in his hands.

This trust, which is the fruit of the union of the will with God and in which this union develops, is not only a feeling of personal security; its object is not ourselves, but it is primarily turned towards him to whom it is addressed, as a testimony of love and a homage of adoration.

Because it is love, it is wholly turned towards him who is the object of this love.

Because it is love, it is gift of self—it is the unconditional surrender of ourselves into the hands of God, in the conviction of belonging to him entirely; it is consent to this total belonging, joy at this total belonging which binds us to him whom we love.

Because it is love, it is effacement of self, it is humility. To love God, to enter into the mystery of his love, is to recognize its entire gratuitousness, to leave in God's hands what the gift of his goodness is to be. It is essentially an attitude of humility.

Thus the path which leads to perfect surrender, to a trustful submission in which the will effaces itself—wholly and completely—before God's will, is a path of humility and patience. Of patience, for suffering is humble. Do we not say 'the humble' to describe the poor, those who suffer?

All poverty, all suffering, all humiliation—all that before which we feel ourselves more powerless, more stripped of everything—all that which hollows out in the soul the void of an entire self-stripping, depriving it of all support—that is what gradually makes it content to remain humbly in God's hands, letting him do with it what he pleases. Humbly, but more and more joyfully, too, as it learns to love this love to which it sees itself entrusted.

It is thus that all suffering, all trials born in a Christian way—in a true Christian spirit, the spirit of the beatitudes, spirit of poverty, spirit of gentleness and peace—makes us share in the mystery of the Cross, a mystery of humility and patience,[1] and thereby, through this very

[1]The collect for Palm Sunday emphasizes this double aspect by showing us in the Passion of Christ an example of humility and a mystery of patience in which we must first of all share, if we are to have a share in the Resurrection.

humility which expands into confidence, brings us to the joy of the resurrection, of the life in God with Christ, in his love.

The joy of a soul risen with Christ. A soul to whom it is enough that God is free to accomplish his will in it, the entirely gratuitous plan of his love.

A soul which no longer knows anything but God. Everything in it is effaced before him. It no longer knows if it desires or hopes, if it is surrendering itself or is submitting; it no longer knows anything except God, and that it must look towards him.

A soul to whom, in each circumstance of its life, it is Christ who comes, and for whom the joy of his resurrection sheds its light more and more strongly on the way of the Cross, which it treads with him.

A soul which can recognize in each of its sufferings and joys Christ who comes to it, a soul who no longer knows anything but the cry of the Christian heart which are the last words of the Scriptures:

Veni, Domine Jesu, Veni.

Conclusion

Conclusion

God first loved us. Everything rests on God's love for us. Our love is only a response.

It is in Christ that this love of the Father is given to us.

For we are one with Christ. And this unity is such that Christ's presence at the right hand of the Father is our assured pledge that our place there is marked out near him. There where he is, we cannot fail to be one day. The life which is in him, his risen life by which he lives in heaven, is not for us an alien, external reality. We have our share in it. It is ours. It is the living reality on which our hope rests—our salvation already achieved, and not just a promise.

The vine is living with unfailing life, and the branch knows that it is drawing from it a life which cannot fail it or disappoint its expectation. It is true that the branch may yet be separated from the vine. But the bond which unites them—the bond which unites us to Christ—carries with it a promise of eternity. It is not a fragile bond. It is strong with the love of Christ for us, with all his fidelity—'My sheep hear my voice . . . I give them eternal life . . . and no one shall snatch them out of my hand.'

The first reality is this divine love towards which our faith must turn—a living faith which will let our life expand in joy, in the joy of confident trust in the strength and endurance of this love.

God loves us and his love has no second thoughts. It is true that he demands a response from us, but in so far as we have understood how true it is to call it a response, we shall be able to understand what sort of response it should be; and this will depend on how firmly our gaze is in the first place fixed on God in an act of faith in the all-powerfulness of his grace, the riches of his mercy.

This faith, very far from being an invitation to slacken our effort, can alone enable us to persevere with firmness and constancy, in security and in peace.

God loves us and asks us to respond to his love. Hence sin is not only an offence against God's justice, it is—in a more profound sense—a refusal of his love.

This is what constitutes the gravity of fully deliberate, clearly accepted, wilful sin. This is what makes us understand also the mercifully compassionate help we may expect from this love which draws us to God and wants us to be his, when our 'refusals' are only the poor, tottering weakness of a will that is sincere, but submerged by so many human attractions which entice it in all directions: 'For the good that I will, I do not, and the evil that I will not, that I do' (Rom., 7, 19).

Let us not however, forget that this will owes it to

itself to be loyal in its strivings. And nothing can be a better encouragement than this thought: just as each of our failures is, in some measure, a refusal of love, so each good impulse is a welcome, an appeal and response to this love. In the face of some temptation more difficult to overcome, or some trial heavier to bear than usual —or simply when confronted with some lack of consideration which it is not at all easy to accept in the serenity of a true charity—the most effective means to overcome our repugnance is surely to learn to discern in the sacrifice thus asked of us, the presence of God's will for us, his will which is love. If then each trial becomes for us an opportunity to exercise ourselves in welcoming this love with joy, under whatever appearance it may offer itself to us, simply because it is God and we have recognized him, the sacrifice will not always be easy on that account, but it will surely be more readily consented to with joy and welcome, without restraint or gloom. It will surely become easier, for instance or, at least, possible to make an act of true patience, of joyful forgiveness, blotting out even the slightest traces of bitterness or resentment, if in this eagerness to give with a good heart all that he asks of us, we see an act of faith in the ever-present love of God, that is held out to us in every circumstance with which he confronts us?

Thus a truly living faith in the love of God will be both our strength in our weakness, enabling us to persevere without weariness or discouragement in a difficult task which reveals our frailty at every step, and the call to a greater generosity, sustained by the joy of total, unreserved, self-giving.

'And we, we have recognized the love God has for us, and we have believed in it' (I John, 4, 16). These words of St John the Apostle express the heart of our Christian faith.